Vision
Of
Change

Vision Of Change

A Caribbean Perspective

JOAN M. PURCELL

2011

authorHOUSE®

AuthorHouse™
1663 Liberty Drive
Bloomington, IN 47403
www.authorhouse.com
Phone: 1-800-839-8640

First published by AuthorHouse—08/10/2011

ISBN: 978-1-4634-3260-7 (sc)
ISBN: 978-1-4634-3259-1 (hc)
ISBN: 978-1-4634-3258-4 (ebk)

Library of Congress Control Number: 2011911935

Printed in the United States of America

Contents

Part I

The Spirituality Of Power And Politics

Part II

Re-Creating Structures:
A Proposal For Caribbean Survival

Part III

Toward A Model Of Wholistic Change

Part IV

Faith, Politics And Leadership

DEDICATION

This work is dedicated to

my son, Don and daughter, Deslin and daughter-in-law Gail,

and to all young leaders of the Caribbean,

who, with eyes of faith, heart of love and feet of hope,

will run with the Vision and make it plain.

ACKNOWLEDGMENTS

How does one begin to thank the hundreds of persons who are involved in the writing of any book? Even when I thought that I was most alone as I wrote, I was simply reflecting the ideas of others whose thoughts have now become my thoughts, whose vision has been incorporated into my vision and whose hopes are now passionately my own.

I am deeply grateful to all those who have travelled this way before me and without whose help, I would still be floundering trying to identify 'who stole my cheese.'

There are two young leaders, who I am privileged to call friends, and to whom I would like to say a public "Thank You"—Ingrid Jackson who is wisely preparing herself for leadership, and Stanley Joseph who like "Barak" does not yet quite accept his calling to lead. I thank these two young leaders who were my earliest critics and ardent supporters as I "tried out" my vision on them.

Special thanks must go to Dr. Wendy Grenade, who graciously wrote the *Foreword*, along with invaluable comments for improving my work and gave me the courage to complete the task; to former Senator Damian Greaves who encouraged me to publish, what is for me, a very daring undertaking, and to the Reverend Doctor Osbert James who painstakingly did the editorial work, showed ongoing solicitude and offered timely support.

Joan M. Purcell

Special thanks also to the several persons who willingly read the manuscript and made valuable comments and suggestions for enhancing the final product.

To my Creator and Father, Author and Finisher, Saviour and Empowerer, the Three-in-One Godhead, I give all honour, glory and thanksgiving, acknowledging that I could do nothing except in His wisdom and strength, and by His grace and mercy.

To God be the Glory!

FOREWORD

Grenada was granted political independence from Britain in 1974 and since independence, two of its Prime Ministers—Herbert Blaize and Sir Nicholas Brathwaite—originated from Carriacou, one of Grenada's sister isles. Less known perhaps is the fact that Carriacou also produced an extraordinary woman—Joan Purcell—whose life characterizes unwavering faith and a passion for service and community. In her public life Joan Purcell has served as a community activist, social worker, child and woman's advocate, development worker, adult educator and member of Grenada's executive and legislature. Currently she is President of the Senate in Grenada.

Purcell has travelled political paths where many others have not dared to tread. In 2007 Joan Purcell shared memoirs of her deepest 'spiritual struggles' as a woman in politics. In that first publication she weaved together an interesting tapestry of political intrigue and faith relevant to Grenada's post-revolutionary political maze.

Memoirs of a Woman in Politics: Spiritual Struggle provides an insider's perspective of political life in Grenada and forces the intellectually curious to reflect on the interplay between spirituality and politics. It also provides lessons on the dynamics of party politics and political leadership and the challenges that confront women in the political process.

Because of these attractive features this book also serves as a useful research text and as well provides a solid foundation for this second publication: *Vision of Change: A Caribbean Perspective.*

Significantly, this book comes at a most critical time in the Caribbean's search for democratic renewal and spiritual awakening. As Caribbean countries, to different degrees, grapple with punctured democracies, economic dislocations, societal insecurities and religious confusion, this book provides a vision for socio-political change grounded in biblical principles.

Purcell is unapologetic about her faith in God and advances a theistic worldview to chart a way forward to a more sustainable future for the Caribbean. Consequently, this book offers a perspective beyond 'accepted' 'politically-correct' worldviews and needs to be appreciated particularly for having a bold conceptual approach to explain the troubled socio-political realities of the Contemporary Caribbean.

All this, of course, is consistent with Purcell's agile, analytic and independent mind, her indomitable courage and practical, strategic activism.

In this book she writes with deep passion and strong conviction. She begins by taking the reader through the malaise that exists in the contemporary Caribbean and proceeds logically and progressively to invite rational response to the dilemma she accurately describes.

What she does really is to invite re-examination of dominant world views in the region and to offer her perspectives for careful intellectual exploration and practical implementation. Purcell continues by interrogating the discourse on democracy in the Caribbean. She posits that while it may be necessary to renew the Westminster model, there is a need to transcend all secular conceptualizations of power itself.

Therefore, pursuing her call for renewal of political philosophical thinking, Purcell unpacks the concept of power and in a novel manner advances perceptively the notion of 'creative, compassionate, reconciling and redeeming' power.

Her radical spiritual lens posits holistic perspectives that challenge the reader profoundly toward having a deeper understanding of the concept of power. But she does not stop at semantics for she proposes strategies.

She offers an alternative for political leadership and socio-political transformation.

Purcell does not describe this book as an academic text. However, it is intellectually stimulating and provokes the reader to transcend traditional paradigms to better understand the complexities of faith, power politics, leadership and community.

As a Political Scientist and a Christian, this book forces me to ask hard questions about discourses in Political Science which privilege Machiavellian notions of power and politics. *Vision of Change: A Caribbean Perspective* offers deep spiritual insights and an alternative lens through which to view the world. It provides a refreshing break from the status quo and offers the possibility of hope and social redemption for Caribbean people. As she so adeptly points out, the path to such an end will not be easy.

Purcell explores other key related concepts such as stewardship and simplicity. She argues that structures need to be re-created for the survival of Caribbean societies. Intriguingly, Purcell draws on her lived experiences and a wide body of literature. Her positive recommendations call for emphasis on concepts such as economic self-reliance, political community and transformed social relations. As she examines the notion of community, she argues that politics builds community, leadership serves community and faith offers transcendence and meaning to community.

She concludes memorably when she declares, 'without faith politics is empty, leadership is shallow, community is impossible, survival is unlikely and chaos is inevitable' (p. 142).

We owe a depth of gratitude to Joan Purcell for reaching so far within herself and outside of herself in analyzing and articulating so ably her deep thoughts and provocative ideas on critical issues for Caribbean survival.

Carriacou, in particular and Grenada on the whole ought to be justifiably proud of this elegant and erudite daughter and passionate Caribbean citizen, for this vision which she has cast as a challenge for us to comprehend and catch in our time of Contemporary Caribbean crisis. Thank you Joan Purcell, as you continue to make your vision our mission

Wendy C. Grenade
Lecturer in Political Science
The University of the West Indies
Cave Hill campus, Barbados.

I will stand my watch

And set my self on the rampart,

And watch to see what He will say to me,

And what I will answer when I am corrected.

Then the Lord answered me and said;

Write the VISION

And make it plain on tablets that he may run who reads it

For the vision is yet for an appointed time;

But at the end it will speak, and it will not lie.

Though it tarries, wait for it; because it will surely come,

It will not tarry.

Behold the proud, his soul is not upright in him;

BUT THE JUST SHALL LIVE BY FAITH.

Habakkuk 2: 1—4

(NKJV)

PREFACE

Almost twenty years ago, I commenced writing on issues of Power, Politics and Change. I was called to public office in 1983 at a particular time of crisis in my country of birth and residence, Grenada, West Indies. Details of my experiences are to be found in my Memoirs (2008).[1] My call to office propelled me to make meaning of the themes of power, politics and change. My reading in this genre widened and deepened. This book is a result of my research and reflections over the past several years and my attempts to shape a vision of change.

Having given birth to my first book three years ago—a work which constituted my personal testimony of a vocational life lived out in the crucible of decision-making, conflict-management and problem-solving within a heated political context, I felt the urgency to resurrect my now dated writings and to update, expand and publish them. Although still involved "in politics," serving in the Parliament of my country as the Presiding Officer of the Senate, I now have more time to reflect, chew upon and digest some of the more important experiences and lessons of the past twenty-five years.

A critique of my memoirs, while lauding its passion, uniqueness and usefulness among Caribbean writing, identifies my failure *"to identify a clear practical path for the spread of revolutionary experience"* that begins in the heart and then spreads to the society. It notes that while the challenge for individual spiritual change is strongly presented, *"it is weak in plotting a path for collective structural change."*[2]

This book is an attempt to begin to expand the vision, to link the personal and the structural, the individual and the societal, the local and the global. It is an invitation for others to join the conversation and an appeal to be invited to the ongoing conversation wherever it is taking place. For me it is a bold *beginning*.

This short book is divided into four parts. Indeed, Part One entitled, "The Spirituality of Power and Politics: A Caribbean Perspective" *(1990)* was included *in part* as the **Epilogue** of my recently published Memoirs. I thought it was a fitting place to begin this new undertaking. Although first written in 1990, so little has changed! My concerns and burdens remain the same; and the relevance of my writings to today's political, social and economic realities in Grenada and elsewhere in the region, I judge to be still appropriate.

Part Two entitled, "Re-creating Structures: A Proposal for Caribbean Survival" was conceived in 1991 and sought briefly to examine the traditional paradigms of socio-economic growth and development and to offer some beginning thoughts on an alternative paradigm.

Part Three entitled, "Toward A Model of Wholistic Change" (1997), seeks to develop a strategy for change and to combine this strategy with some recommended practice intended to assist in effectively communicating this vision for change.

Parts one, two and three have been updated and expanded. Part Four entitled, "Faith, Politics and Leadership," brings together for me three significant themes which constitute a life of service in the public domain. The interrelatedness of these themes and how each impact and give meaning to the other will be underscored, and their relevance to today's political environment will be highlighted.

Each of the parts of this work can stand on its own and may be read based on personal appeal and interest. It is my hope though that each part will give greater insight, clarity and meaning to the other.

For me, these perspectives are constantly honed, refined and transformed as I'm permitted to look into the hearts and minds of other writers whose passion and compassion I share. I lay no claim to the originality of ideas that over time have become a part of my own consciousness. Scores of writers and scholars have contributed to this work, though only a few have been acknowledged. I am deeply grateful.

It is hoped that at least one of the consequences of these ideas will be to communicate the urgent need for Caribbean people to redeem the time, to intensify the dialogue, and to speed up the pace of refining our vision and mission so as to provide meaningful hope to a largely youthful population.

I wish to state that when I allude to "Caribbean people," I speak specifically of the Anglophone or English—speaking Caribbean, from the Bahamas in the North to Guyana in the South.

This group of countries is among those classified by the United Nations as Small Island Development States (SIDS) as they share similar sustainable development challenges, including small populations, limited resources, susceptibility to natural disasters, vulnerability to external shocks and excessive dependence on international trade. Growth and development are often stymied by high transportation and communication costs, disproportionally expensive public administration and infrastructure due to small size and little or no opportunities to create economies of scale. (UN Department of Economic and Social Affairs, Division of Sustainable Development).[3]

This group of Anglophone Caribbean countries also shares a common political history of colonialism, "chattel slavery of Afro Caribbean people and indentured labourers from Asia."[4] Now considered postcolonial societies, the majority now enjoy political independence, have adapted a Westminster model of governance characterized by a parliamentary form of democracy. Wendy Grenade commenting on issues confronting these democracies observed:

> Yet, despite the trappings of democratic forms and procedures, Caribbean Democracies are bedeviled by authoritarian tendencies, corruption within the state; clientelism; tribalism; gender imbalances and a general disconnect between the

> citizen and the state . . . the Caribbean political culture is based primarily on state-centrism, paramountcy of the party and prime ministerial abuse of power. The nature of governance thus undermines trust, distorts identity and provides limited space for genuine citizen engagement and community participation.[5]

It is within and on the basis of the above historical and present day context that I wish to cast a vision of socio-political change.

My hope is that this book will become a useful text for discussion, reflection, analysis and action for leaders and managers, teachers and students, visionaries and activists, pastors and priests, politicians and policymakers, professionals and practitioners, as they seek to examine wide ranging options and differing perspectives on transformational possibilities for our region.

May this work redound to the good of Caribbean people and the Glory of God.!

Introduction: The Call for a Vision of Change

Everything that is happening in our world is saying we are going the wrong way.

Darrell Johnson

This book comes out of years of reflection and often solitary debate on the state of the world in general and the Caribbean Region in particular, enhanced by political and social experience in the Parliament of my country as well as in the market place of life.

While this work may not be justifiably considered a scholarly, formally researched thesis or treatise, nevertheless it is rooted in reliable, creditable literature review, and real life experiences observed and lived. What therefore has been produced is not merely descriptive for analytic conclusions are definitely prescriptive.

Twenty years ago, in a publication entitled, *Storm Signals: Structural Adjustment and Development Alternatives in the Caribbean,* Kathy McAfee[6] noted the ominous trends emerging within a region marked by extreme openness, with unusually high-dependence on imports and exports, features that made the region especially vulnerable to external political pressures and changing conditions that cannot be internally controlled. Also noted was the small size of the region which was perceived to have deleterious consequences, for that allowed little bargaining power in negotiations over trade, investment and lending.

The crisis in the Caribbean was seen by her then, to reflect growing urbanization and destruction of rural economies as more and more persons drift to cities to find jobs; trade patterns dependent on the exchange of unprocessed agricultural and mineral commodities for imported manufactured products and basic consumer goods; lack of control over export prices which would lead more and more to balance of trade deficits and high levels of external debt.

McAfee's powerfully perceptive observations were devastating concerning Caribbean reality: "the single most important reality that underlies the poverty and dependency of the Caribbean is the lack of connection between the uses of the region's resources—land, water, minerals, and human knowledge and labor—and the real needs and desires of the region's people. "[7]

McAfee's comments two decades ago provide a telling explanation why today the needs of Caribbean people remain largely unmet. So little has changed over the years to seriously and sustainably address those issues! The problems have in fact been exacerbated, the challenge for constructive change multiplied, and the opportunities for creative change contracted by the recent crisis of international capital.

The critical nature of these concerns has not of course gone unnoticed. Throughout the region voices are raised, from the politician to the professor to the pastor—the Caribbean is in crisis!

In a position paper by Senator Christopher De Allie, representative of the Private Sector in the Parliament of Grenada: "*Global Economic Crisis and its Consequences for the Region*"(2009), the reality of the situation in which we find ourselves today is underscored:

> Our economies consist largely of small-island states with open but fragile economies based on a limited number of commodities which make us vulnerable and highly influenced by developments in the world economy . . . the global crisis will exacerbate some of the underlying problems inherent within Caribbean economies, such as openness to international trade, reliance on certain exports, and heavy indebtedness. Some pre-existing social problems, particularly in relation to poverty, restricted employment opportunities, and crime, will surely pose greater challenges . . . . We need stability, fortitude, unity and a strong sense of purpose to see us through these difficult times.[8]

Grenadian/Caribbean Political Scientist and University Lecturer, Wendy Grenade reflects:

Almost fifty years after the collapse of the West Indies Federation and the journey toward Independence, Caribbean countries, individually and collectively, continue to confront serious challenges to their politics, economies and societies . . . they continue to grapple, to varying degrees, with poverty, indebtedness, illiteracy, high prevalence of HIV/AIDS, environmental vulnerability, crime and violence and deficiencies in governance, which threaten human, social and economic development.[9]

Jamaican Evangelical Pastor and Media Commentator, Reverend Garnett Roper, in describing the present Caribbean moment, in particular Jamaica's, made the following observation:

There is little doubt that this is a region and a society in severe crisis. The rate of violent crimes, especially murder has created a climate of instability and fear. The effect of the global realities in the global financial systems as well as the inheritance of high national debt and fiscal imprudence has put the livelihoods of the majority of citizens at risk . . . In addition social exclusion and social inequality have been deepening and are exacerbated among Caribbean people. Jamaica for example has sixty per cent of its high school cohort leaving schools without passing a single subject . . . . The society has become accustomed to more than twenty percent of its youth male population becoming gang members, there is high unemployment among young women. This has led to a higher incidence of public disorder and social dysfunctionality.[10]

In a "Situation Analysis of women and children in the Eastern Caribbean" done by UNICEF (2007), it is noted that "the economies of the sub-region are among the most vulnerable in the world".[11] Antigua/Barbuda was ranked as the second most vulnerable country out of the 111 countries on the Commonwealth Vulnerability Index; Grenada ranked 15. Besides the unenviable position of being located in a natural disaster-prone zone, a major reason for our vulnerability is that our macroeconomic and fiscal policies "have often been a source of vulnerability rather than remedy."[12] The study flagged poverty as a major issue noting that "Poverty is a problem in the sub-region despite the fact that the countries have reached a level of development that should allow a significant proportion of the poor to escape from poverty. "[13]

The UNICEF analysis noted that unemployment rates are high, especially among women and youth, with the average unemployment rate for the sub-region of the Eastern Caribbean being about 12 percent men and 16 percent women. Teenage mothers account for between 10 to 20 percent of live births in several of the islands. An estimated 5,100 persons are living with HIV in the OECS region, where the average incidence is approaching 0.1 percent, the second highest in the world. AIDS is now the leading cause of death in the age group 15—to 44.[14]

Crime rates are soaring in all the islands of the region, increasing in frequency and gruesomeness of the crime. The number of recorded murders for Jamaica for 2009 was 1680, by May 2010, 609 murders were reported. It was said by the Commissioner of Police of Jamaica that what he described as a "*crime/politics nexus*" existed in his country, compounded by trans-national organized crime.[15] In Grenada in April/May 2010, a woman was stabbed four times at the door of her church; two days later a young man in his thirties was arrested for the beheading of two of his village acquaintances.[16]

Family violence is a challenge in all states and reported incidences of child abuse is said to be escalating at an alarming rate. A study on "Perceptions of Child Sexual Abuse" in several islands of the Eastern Caribbean, while noting what appears to be its prevalence and acceptance, laments the absence of "collective outrage." [17]

Dr. Wendy Grenade, in an analysis of the present Caribbean environment, noted that "the high incidence of crime and violence threaten societal safety, undermine human security, and impede economic growth and social development." [18] We have spawned a "culture of violence" which goes directly against the image of the Caribbean as a peaceful and idyllic place of beauty and social cohesion.

Our communities are in crisis. Indeed, in a Resurrection Day Message on April, 04, 2010, Grenadian Pastor, the Reverend Christopher Baker declared, *"our communities are decaying."*[19] Some of our communities have become "garrison communities," the hub of crime, violence and partisan politics defying all attempts at law and order. Training Consultant and Community Specialist, Dr. Patricia Ellis, in commenting on her recent work in conducting poverty assessments among Eastern Caribbean countries notes the dehumanization and debilitation which presently characterize Caribbean communities: old ties have unravelled, competitiveness and acquisitiveness abound, and apathy and alienation are the order of the day.[20]

Parents have become powerless, the church has lost its distinctiveness, politics characterless, education appears pointless, and even the West Indies cricket team—the pride of Caribbean people—experience severely limited success and has lost its place of regional attractiveness.

Our very foundations are being destroyed!

In the words of Grenade, "What we are witnessing is a shift away from communities towards individualism, materialism, greed, intolerance, ill-discipline and mediocrity. This reflects a larger spiritual paralysis and societal abyss".[21]

The Caribbean region is in jeopardy of losing its soul, if that has not already happened.

The Anglophone Caribbean and I speak particularly without intending to be insular, urgently needs a new Vision of Change. It is my intention to join the ongoing conversation in shaping such a vision for the Region.

I wish to state clearly that I write from the particular perspective of an afro-Caribbean woman, a believer in and follower of Jesus Christ, a development activist/Adult Educator and a Community/Political Leader. My view of the world is therefore shaped and presented within the framework and particularities of the above roles.

Permit me to spend sometime exploring the phenomenon of worldviews and how important they are in the shaping of our vision of change and transformation.

A worldview is the lens through which individually we see the world. The essential thing about a worldview perspective is that it provides us with meaning for all that is happening to and around us. This world view provides us with a story—a story which gives rise to our culture, the way we live, the way we make meaning, the way we view reality, the way we define transformation and define ourselves in this transformative process.

I rather like the way Darrell Johnson puts it: 'Every culture has its 'metanarrative', its 'deep story' which seeks to make sense of life. The story or worldview is that set of glasses through which a culture looks at the world. Every 'deep story' circles around the key questions: Who are we? Where are we? What's wrong? What's the solution? And what time is it?"[22]

My own awareness and understanding of the crucial significance of worldviews came from my reflection and study of the work of Darrow L. Miller, a social activist, development worker and strong proponent of a biblical worldview. Permit me therefore to draw heavily on his work in his seminal book, *"Discipling Nations: The Power of Truth to transform cultures"*[23]. In that book he states:

> All people and cultures have a particular model of the universe, or worldview. Their worldview does more to shape their development, their prosperity or poverty, than does their physical environment or other circumstances . . . each worldview creates different cultural stories and produces different values. Ideas produce behaviours and lifestyles that affect people, cultures, nations and history.[24]

As I join the continuing dialogue on Caribbean social reality, I will confine myself to a brief overview of three worldview archetypes: animism, humanism (secularism) and biblical theism.

ANIMISTIC WORLD VIEW

In the animistic world view reality is essentially framed as spiritual. Miller describes it in this way:

The physical world is' maya', illusion. It is "animated" by spirits. Animism (including its modern form, the New Age) is rooted in the Far East and the world's folk religions. Spirits animate everything, and every thing moves toward oneness of spirit. The real world is unseen, truth is hidden and irrational, all is mystery. While filled with evil, the universe is basically amoral. Monistic, animism asserts that there is only one kind of ultimate substance. The animist might cry, "All is one!" This is philosophical idealism, which maintains that ultimate reality lies in a realm that transcends worldly phenomenon; essentially, reality is consciousness.[25]

HUMANISTIC WORLD VIEW (Secularism)

Secularism, on the opposite end of the continuum, sees reality as ultimately physical. It denies the reality of the spiritual or transcendent. Ultimate reality focuses on the unity of nature. Miller states:

Darwin, one of the great high priests of secularism, believed that life is the result of the interactions of matter and energy, time and chance. Secularists affirm that truth is empirical. Truth is what senses perceive. Morals are relative. Values emerge from social consensus. . . . The cry of the secularist might be, "Everything is God!" This is philosophical materialism. Matter is the only and fundamental reality; all being, processes and phenomenon are explained as manifestations of matter. During the Enlightenment these ideas received the label "secular humanism".[26]

While both animism and secularism tell a part of the story, they do not tell the whole story. There is a *transforming* story—one that today is rarely fully explored in all its transcendent and transformational possibilities.

THEISTIC WORLD VIEW

The theistic world view or theism, even more specifically biblical theism, falls between the above two, is rooted in the ancient Near East. Miller posits:

It sees ultimate reality as personal and relational. **God exists**. He created a universe of physical and spiritual dimensions, seen and unseen worlds. Truth, as revealed by God, is objective and can be known by man. God's character establishes absolute morals. Theism holds to one personal-infinite God, the great "I AM" of Scripture. Philosophical theism believes that the one God created man and the world. God transcends the world yet is immanent in it.[27] [emphasis mine].

Worldviews are not static. They spread horizontally, between and among people. These ideas also penetrate vertically into the various spheres of life and become institutionalized in the laws of the society, the politics and the social and economic structures, the pop culture, the village life and affect lifestyle and life choices. Worldviews also diffuse through time and with modern information technology, ideas—good and bad—spread swiftly. The fundamental lesson on worldviews is that ideas have consequences.

I therefore submit that an understanding of worldviews in any discussion on the creation of a vision for the Caribbean is indispensable. An examination of the basic worldview that informs *modern* Caribbean systems, structures and policies will reveal a secular humanistic/materialistic approach often couched in theological language.

The Caribbean, as a product of European colonization, has always primarily reflected the worldview of the imperial powers. The worldview of Theism, having its roots in Judeo—Christianity of the Ancient Near East was traditionally the predominant view of the West. This worldview assumed "a transcendent, infinite, personal God Who existed before all else".[28] God is seen to be immanent, meaning He is present within creation, and transcendent, visible outside of creation. God who is everywhere present and involved operates in an open system, open to His purpose and intervention. This Supreme Being of the Universe revealed Himself in His written word, the Bible, and in the Living Word, Jesus Christ. Here, God is seen at work in history. Indeed all history is seen as His story.

The prevailing theistic worldview of the West began to disintegrate and of course impacted far and wide on nations and countries within its orbit—its sphere of influence. I wish to quote at some length Miller's description of this disintegrating process:

> The consensus for this worldview began crumbling in Europe and England during the Age of the Enlightenment. Intellectuals of the time were seeking to free man **from** God's authority and established dogmas and free man **for** his own autonomy. One manifestation of this shift was **deism**, in which God was seen as transcendent but not immanent. The deist's God created the universe and founded the natural law. Like a clock maker, God wound up the universe and allowed it to run its course. Not surprisingly, the Age of Enlightenment saw the birth of rationalism. The universe was viewed as a machine with man at the center. Because God is not immanent in this model, special revelation is excluded, and man cannot know Him personally. However, people can use their rationality to grasp the existence of God, along with the natural laws God has built into the universe.
>
> Atheistic materialism, or secularism, brought the process one more step. If God does not communicate with man and is not immanent, why do we need a god at all? The revolt of autonomous man was nearly complete by the end of the nineteenth and beginning of the twentieth centuries. Man was alone in an impersonal, mechanical universe. Secularism was unfolded in every area of life, and materialism came to dominate the West. Man was now free from all absolutes, able to decide what is true and false, right and wrong. Without God, there was no revelation. While man may reason, there is nothing transcendent to discover.[29]

This worldview of modern man, modern humanism, impacted education through Darwinism, and spread its virulence to every aspect of life, including religion, creating a divide between the sacred and the secular. Dualism emerged, dividing the sacred from the secular. Politics became secular, while spirituality became sacred, and never the twain shall meet.

Today modernity and post modernity impact the fundamentals of our culture, our economics, our family, our communities, our notions of development and transformation. Modern man turned in upon himself, seeking answers that could not be found in oneself—the tragedy of modernity and the tragedy of nations like the Caribbean, locked in the sphere of influence of the Western world that is itself disintegrating.

The theistic worldview formed the basis of the early beginnings of a Caribbean culture.

It is the view of many that Missionaries who came to the Caribbean to 'spread the gospel message,' came with a dualistic, contaminated, worldview, one that, had moved away from the early apostolic tradition. What emerged was further penetrated by syncretism of aspects of African culture which came with slavery and which was more animistic in nature. Caribbean culture remains officially theistic (we are described as 'Christian nations") and all significant institutions—laws, government, family, and religion—give assent to belief in a Sovereign, Supreme God of the Universe.

The shift of worldviews in the West propelled a gradual shift in the worldview of the Caribbean region and today though many of our institutions and systems retain a faint theistic fragrance, the formulas, prescriptions, policies and plans, goals and strategies for the ongoing growth and development of the region give out a powerful odor of modern day materialism and secularism, confused by an occasional whiff of animistic spiritualism and compounded by an intolerant smell of dualism. Is it any wonder that it is not working for us? Scripture defines it as " . . . *a form of godliness, but denying the power thereof*" (2Timothy 3:5, KJV).

In order to explore more fully how worldviews impact on our way of life, permit me to spend sometime examining from a worldview perspective, the issue of poverty—the significant reduction of which constitutes a major challenge to all Caribbean nations.

But before I go any further may I present three classifications of poverty as found in the literature I have consulted, namely the *indigent poor* deprived of basic necessities, the *oppressed poor*, described as powerless victims of human injustice, and the *humble poor* who acknowledge their helplessness and look to God to supply their needs.[30]

Poverty when discussed from the perspective of the Caribbean, describes *the indigent* poor (those whose income is less than US$1,000 per annum) and *the poor* whose income is under US$2,000 per annum. Poverty levels of *the poor* range from about 12 percent in Barbados to 37 percent in Grenada, and 38 percent in St. Vincent and the Grenadines.[31]

Why are our Caribbean nation states — with some of the richest soils on earth, an abundance of fruit, vegetables and vegetation, exotic spices found no where else in the world, with some of the most beautiful beaches—a miracle combination of sun, sea and sand, available fresh water, marine and mineral resources, manageable population densities, a rich cultural heritage from the diverse races of people living together in relative harmony, a long tradition of democracy and representative government — remained among the poorest nations of the world?

Much of our analysis on the roots of poverty in a society sees it as external to the society.

We blame it on exploitation of colonialism/neo-colonialism or Western consumerism or capitalist imperialism based on the world view of the "revolutionary secularist" (Marxist/Socialist). Or we may blame it on lack of or insufficient natural and financial resources, and rising population growth, the viewpoint of the "evolutionary secularist" (Capitalist).

Miller submits that "both the evolutionary and revolutionary positions stem from a materialistic point of view. Hunger and poverty is seen primarily in physical terms in nature, in the environment, in circumstances. Both view nature in a closed system. The problem is defined in material terms, and the solution . . . framed in material terms."[32]

And while very, very strong arguments may be made (and these are not ignored within the pages of this work) that developing countries like the Caribbean have been exploited by unjust and unfair trade patterns, governments have been corrupt and inept and have ignored the poor and the vulnerable, commerce and multinational/transnational corporations have been inordinately greedy and excessive in their profit making pursuits, that Europe has indeed left Africa and the Caribbean undeveloped—while all of these are powerful facts for the systemization of poverty — the analysis remains incomplete and the solutions unsustainable. If the enemy of poverty remains *only* external, all our Millennium Development Goals are doomed to fail.

ALTERNATIVE WORLD VIEW

I wish to move now to what a theistic approach, an alternative viewpoint and worldview, adds to the analysis of the situation of poverty, where billions in our world find themselves trapped with little relief in sight. Around the world, thirty thousand children die daily from lack of clean drinking water and a basic meal. In Latin America and the Caribbean 51 million people (9 million under the age of five) were estimated undernourished (hungry) in 2007.[33] A theistic position submits that external conditions, while engendering and entrenching poverty, do not alone create and sustain poverty. It argues, further, that while poverty is both systemic and structural, it is also deeply personal!

It insists, that indeed a deeply entrenched contributor to poverty and one most difficult to eliminate is that of "a poverty of the mind" which is premised on a worldview that sees oneself in a closed system, totally incapable of escape, totally dependent on a less than benign outside world and finite human forces to bring freedom and to bring change for the better.

Myles Munroe, one of the Caribbean's strongest proponents of a path of responsible freedom as the Caribbean's route to authentic liberty, offers his propositions on the basis of a biblical, theistic worldview. He traces the lives of Third World peoples, including the Caribbean, from a condition of slavery and oppression to paths of democratic freedom, which have not resulted in mental freedom and transformation of Caribbean peoples. He argues that "nothing changes until your mind changes."[34] He acknowledges that "though oppression begins as an external experience, the ultimate effect is the resulting mental and psychological bondage."[35] Munroe insist that while several Caribbean countries are rich in natural resources they remain poor nations, victims of international capital and mentally enslaved to an oppressive past. From a biblical worldview, he posits:

> Freedom cannot be legislated. It is the result of revelation knowledge of one's true self and value . . . a delivered body does not guarantee a free mind. The only road to true freedom is self discovery in God the Creator, and the prescribed way to Father God is through His Son, Jesus Christ . . . (Who) when speaking of true freedom . . . said . . . "You will know the truth, and the truth will set you free . . . if the Son sets you free, you will be free indeed." (John 8:32 & 36 NIV). [36]

A theistic analysis in examining the issue of poverty and other such conditions begins with a Sovereign God Who created a world of fruitfulness and abundance and declared it all good. A theistic worldview begins with the Supreme God of the Universe creating humans—a man and a woman—in His own image and likeness. A woman and man who were given the mandate to cultivate and care for God's good earth! A man and woman who were charged with being faithful stewards of a rich, fertile and ecologically balanced environment!

In a theistic worldview man and woman rebelled against a Holy God—indeed chose to take control of their own lives. Human beings became alienated from God and His blessings. Man sinned against God and set in train humanity's drift from the rich supply of God's bounty to the poverty, meagreness and hardship of a life without God set in motion by the injunction: *"by the sweat of your brow you will eat food"* (Genesis 3: 19 NIV).

The consequences of man's separation from God became inevitable: Your toil will be painful; your rewards meager, the ground unyielding and your end death. Therein is the deepest source of human poverty! Man's inhumanity to man, human greed and corruption, inhumane and unjust systems and structures are all symptoms of the underlying problem of spiritual poverty, in other words godlessness. Changing man's environment and circumstances *alone* will not deal with the insidious evil of mental and spiritual poverty. And that is what we seek to do utilizing a materialistic-humanistic approach to development and transformation.

But alas, we do not give up. Indeed, we have cause to rejoice—the "audacity of hope" is alive. The tenacity of faith is available. And the generosity of love is accessible. The theistic story did not end with the rebellion of humans leading to poverty, bondage and death. Indeed a new story immediately unfolded. The Sovereign God set in motion a perfect plan to redeem fallen humankind, to restore divine fellowship and to replenish healthy bounty.

TRANSFORMATIONAL DEVELOPMENT

Miller talks of "transformational development" as a logical consequence of the theistic worldview—this kind of change, he says, "impacts both man's spirit and man's body . . . This transformation begins on the inside at the level of beliefs and values, and moves outward to embrace behaviour and its consequences. Transformational development is a dynamic process." [37]

It begins by accepting the truth of Who God is and the need of humans to experience God's provision for redemption and reconciliation to restore the broken relationship between Creator and creature, between human and human, between human and his/her environment. This *true* truth impacts on systems and structures, institutions and societies. It creates visions of change. It ushers in a new world of relationships, a new brand of community and a new way to live.

In this book it is my contention that today, the greatest tragedy of our world is that those of us who avowedly support a theistic worldview, propound an incomplete, often distorted and tragically compromised view of the world, thereby contributing to the strengthening of systems that strangle so much of human creativity and initiative, that stifle the enormous potential and possibilities of a humanity possessing the image and likeness of God, and having access to the redeeming, reconciling power of Christ Jesus through the Spirit of God.

The burden of the work is to bring transcendence and theistic spirituality back into humanity—its politics, economics, development and culture. It is also to reaffirm the existence of the Sovereign, Supreme Godhead, Creator and Sustainer of history—a history that is going somewhere.

The intent of this presentation is to affirm the dignity and admit the depravity of humans whom God has chosen to be co-creators of His wonder-filled universe, acting as trustworthy stewards of the environment, servant leaders of nations, responsible citizens in communities, faithful partners in families—makers of peace, ambassadors of reconciliation, models of transformation, and creators of vision and builders of communities and missionaries to spiritually lost humanity.

I have, so far, found little published work in the Caribbean positing a theistic or biblical worldview for understanding and interpreting our contemporary political economy and history. My research to date has yielded little in terms of writing attempting to prescribe a way forward for a more sustainable future. My ambitious attempt may therefore seem to some persons an uninitiated and unwelcome "voice crying in the wilderness". Yet, I have with deliberation decided to venture forth courageously, for I am convinced that from all that I have found, there is sufficient to justify proposing what I have done in the hope of encouraging others to join in the casting of a vision of Caribbean social reality with admirable possibility.

Jim Wallis in discussing the marks of an emerging prophetic vision warns (and I wholeheartedly agree with him) that there are no blueprints or ideological manifesto, but there are core values, spiritual guideposts and road maps to guide in this journey of a new vision. He explains:

> Such visions must be both spiritual and political and must have concrete social, economic, and cultural consequences. New visions are usually expressed in movements . . . they more often originate from the margins and the bottom . . . . indeed, it is the moral failure of our powerful institutions and the ethical poverty of our successful elites that will create the need for new visions and possibilities . . . Vision comes more by renewal than by reaction. The deepest changes come from a revolution of the spirit rather than a revolution of the gun. Hope has always been a more powerful force for change than despair . . . . underneath failed social values, corrupted institutions, and destructive personal behaviour is a reservoir of moral conscience. Our

religious traditions call that "the image of God" stamped on our hearts. At the same time (we have been shown).the depths to which humanly conceived evil and brutality can go. The Bible calls that our "fallenness". It is the appeal to the image of God within us that is the most persuasive weapon against human fallenness. New social visions are forged by such an appeal. [38]

This book is one such attempt to sound an appeal for a new political vision. The contents that follow seek to explore and engage our minds at the depths to which our institutions have fallen, especially the institution of politics. Some core values are resurrected, spiritual guideposts explored and road maps examined.

It will be vain to pretend that I have answered all the thorny questions, simplified the deep complexities and explained all the confusing paradoxes of life lived on this planet in these few pages. Others have tried. But only God can provide all the answers and He has chosen not to do so.

Nevertheless, it is my hope though that this book will encourage you to re-examine your worldview and to explore—really explore what lies beneath the way you think. I pray that you will be moved to call forth the awesome possibilities and potentialities of being human, "made in the image and likeness of God"; that you will be encouraged to transcend the natural inclination to fallenness, and to accept the challenge of reconciliation and restoration offered by the Sovereign Godhead.

A theistic worldview is the lens through which I have sought to understand, analyze and interpret our world and our region, and I invite fellow travellers to join me as we listen together to the "still, small voice of God" as He works through us to restore lost years, rebuild broken down walls and erect new highways of love, faith and hope.

PART 1

THE SPIRITUALITY OF POWER AND POLITICS:

A CARIBBEAN PERSPECTIVE

POLITICAL POWER: THE CARIBBEAN DILEMMA

Power that is no longer exercised under God seeks to play God.

Darrell Johnson

The struggle for political power in the lands of the contemporary Caribbean has been disheartening. It is a tale of woe, compounded by economic and industrial unrest, interpersonal and racial conflicts, street violence, criminal activities such as drug trafficking and kidnapping, national rebellion and revolution. In this part of the world, comprised mostly but not entirely of island-states, parliamentary principles and constitutional processes have been perverted and derailed. Political leadership has undermined people-power through personal charisma, intellectual snobbery, deliberate mystification and party manipulation. Underlying the façade of nevertheless touted success is a system of graft, corruption and institutional deceit. Evidently, the cause of democracy has been ill served by persons declaring commitment to gaining and keeping political power while in reality accomplishing no more than the support and maintenance of the 'status quo'.

Consequently, Caribbean people have become, in general, disillusioned and disenchanted with their political realities. After decades of mostly 'dashed' hopes, the rhetoric of politicians today is greeted with much apathy, muted indifference and at times scepticism and even cynicism. In some instances politicians are made to feel the pervasive pessimism that is packaged with insults and even rudeness. Yet, strangely, every five years or so hundreds of thousands of nationals continue to go through the oftentimes violent process that involves campaigning expensively and then casting unwisely a ballot to put a party 'in power'. However noticeably, once that seemingly distasteful task of voting is done, the majority of citizenry retreat into political apathy marked by non-involvement and unreasonable expectations! In some instances, there are individuals who organize chicanery, but most persons retreat to engaging in what may be termed broadly, living a life of indifference to transformational possibilities.

The ruling party ascends with pomp and pageantry and then proceeds to flout the newly acquired authority they once espoused to despise. The now chastened 'Opposition,' both official and unofficial, proceeds to systematically discredit whatever good, bad or indifferent programs that the party in office chooses to announce or attempt. In that regard they tend to have dependable allies among some influential groups in the community. In that social situation among deprived, underdeveloped Caribbean people, the spoils of victory are expected to go to winners and their adherents while members of the 'defeated' community retreat into bitterness and disinterest. The consequence is that the best interest of the people is abandoned in favour of a pervasive spirit of negativity and divisiveness and underdevelopment and poverty remain persistent allies of our rapidly aging democracies.

In regard to this assessment, I found the work of Caribbean scholar, David Hinds'[39] in his discourse on Democracy and Governance in the Anglophone Caribbean to be extremely useful in corroborating my own personal insights and even more importantly in providing an analysis drawn from the work of notable regional scholars on the state of parliamentary democracy and governance in our nation states. Permit me, therefore to draw attention to some significant comments and conclusions from this paper.

One of the significant observations he made is that while it was generally agreed by several Caribbean scholars that the Westminster model of democracy that characterized our pre and post independence eras had provided some significant level of constitutional order and stability in the region, except for the experiments of Guyana (1968-1992) and Grenada ((1979-1983), it had not contributed to the expected political, social and economic equality and advancement. Hinds remarks:

> Instead, the antidemocratic culture that characterized the pre-independence order, despite some modifications at the time of independence, has persisted in the post-colonial era . . . It can also reasonably be argued that there has, in our region, been too destructive a competition for political office; too heavy a concentration of power in the hands of the ruling elites, an unhealthy preservation of anti-development party

and tribal division, a focus on short term partisan political concerns rather than long-term strategic objectives, and efficient patronage and spoils systems which work against sound and progressive government. Alienation, cynicism and marginalization have been the result, all leading to a perpetuation of underdevelopment.[40]

Not surprisingly then, in light of the limited success of the Westminster Model in the Caribbean to advance quality of life generally and maturity in politics in particular, there is a growing call for at least significant modification of our Westminster system, along with introduction of alternative electoral processes.

Of course, there is general acknowledgment that our inherited system of governance has led to increased democratization of the political structures and broad-based participation by the people of the Caribbean in our post-independence period. But it is also true that under this form of governance, marked characteristically by political party winner taking all the spoils, there is no adequate basis for hoping to see within a reasonably short time the desired and desirable social transformation of our small societies.

While I wholeheartedly agree that the Caribbean needs to seriously examine and reform its present model of governance, to be committed only to structural modification of the system tightens our entrapment to the lie that systemic change by itself can bring about the crucially needed fundamental change. Let's take for example the idea of 'Proportional Representation' now considered by many as a significant alternative. While 'Proportional Representation' as an electoral process, could, no doubt, contribute to the lessening of the present alienation of Opposition parliamentarians and parties and allow more persons to benefit from the process of electoral politics, but important questions relating to this *structural* change remain to be seriously addressed.

One such critical question would be whether such a modification is, as necessary as it may be, sufficient to foster a mindset of independence/interdependence among Caribbean peoples? In other words, would such a strategy provide sufficient inducement and motivation to move Caribbean people to adequately accept the full responsibility of freedom that leads to social transformation?

Indeed the question needs to be posed again and again, would it result in a more creative way of understanding and using *power*? After all, what we are desiring in terms of the vision being cast is a qualitative shift in the way we define ourselves and make meaning of our lives and this can only come about by the way we see ourselves and our world—our worldview.

From where we are at this point in our history, there is urgent need for a re-examination of the philosophical thinking which has so far driven all efforts at change and transformation in our region. Urgently, we need those who will accept this challenge to current thinking. Perhaps the best hope we might entertain in this regard is that Caribbean leaders and scholars will accept the challenge, the urgent and important challenge for a shift in worldview, as they are the ones who through dissemination of ideas fundamentally influence the change process. Indeed, "ideas have consequences".[41]

But can we put our hope in our intellectual elite? We too often have to admit that the coded language of academia is unintelligible to the majority of everyday sufferers and not intended for the comprehension of ordinary citizens. Furthermore, most of the work of our 'brightest' scholars is based on the humanistic-secularist agenda—a materialistic worldview of life.

Could we look to our religious leaders? In regard, to our religious leaders from whom we seek moral and spiritual direction, unlike the men of Issachar who understood the times and therefore knew what to do (1Chronicles 12:32), they have given up on our institutions, our God-given institutions, and have failed to be "salt" and light", infiltrating and impacting the society with the light of the Kingdom of God and the salt of ethical morality on cutting issues. In truth, Caribbean people, by and large, seem to have abandoned the Church as the institution of hope for social upliftment, and have turned toward political parties and politicians for redemption leadership. Is this where we went wrong? It is a valid question and a probing one. For so wholeheartedly was our shift from religion to politics as our source of well-being that we can be scored for not recognizing or refusing to accept that politicians to whom we entrusted so much of our hopes had feet of clay and knees of weakness.

Today, our politicians are seriously compromised; our intellectuals ideologically confused; and our religious leaders lacking in courage. Of course, there are exceptions—notable exceptions.

Our concern at this time however is our capacity to endure the consequences of our failures brought on by the falsity and hypocrisy of our patterns of behaviour that have maintained the people of this region in a spiralling stage of underdevelopment.

What then must we do? As Caribbean peoples, we need to say like the prodigal in the far country, it is time to stop and take stock. We need to re-assess ourselves in regard to the road we have taken. We need to embark on careful stock-taking of our political, social, religious and cultural realities. And we need to do so now, for time is running out for us. Therefore, we must wake up from our 'historical amnesia' and recognize that all is far from well—we dare not be complaisant. We are scattered geographically but united in confusion over our identity and the poverty of our reality. We are a people in moral retreat.

Consequently, most of our people are apathetic and alienated. In this very dangerous situation we are vulnerable. This means in practical terms that we are in danger of moving from bad to worse. This is because when in such a parlous state desperate people tend to succumb all too readily to expediency over principle. But the easy path ought never to be encouraged. We must fight back to achieve victory. We must resist the temptation to seek easy solutions. We must be prepared to accept the radical, as may be necessary, for us to move forward. But radical must be hastily interpreted not as that which might be imposed with bombs and bullets.

To begin our march toward a new day of hope for the Caribbean let us be clear about our first step. Let us begin to re-conceptualize our understanding of 'power'. At the heart of much of our distress and confusion is the use and misuse of *power*. Socio-political change is really about the power relationships among people. It is about how power is defined used and shared. Therefore, let us proceed to explore the concept of power we have and the concept of power we need to have.

'Power' as commonly explained in dictionaries is a concept that includes *the ability to act; the exercise of a faculty of strength; the exercise of any kind of control, dominion, sway, command, government;* and *the ability to do or to act.* Dictionaries, of course, report meanings in use, and one way to make sense of meanings is to distinguish between kinds. A very helpful definition that distinguishes thus is provided by Richard Foster, who says: "power can destroy or create. The power that destroys demands ascendancy; it demands total control. It destroys relationships . . . trust . . . dialogue . . . integrity. The power that creates is spiritual power, the power that proceeds from God. Creative power sets people free . . . produces unity . . . it is in stark contrast to human power."[42] Accepting that delineating definition of power, the one that finds endorsement and so selective focus for this discussion is the creative, liberating power that even though radical is the power needed to hopefully lead to desirable Caribbean social transformation. Therefore, this is the concept that will be pursued in this discussion.

POWER: HUMANIZED AND COMPROMISED

Radical problems can be effectively tackled by radical thinking and acting. Therefore a radical concept of power is needed to counter the debilitating despair of current social realities in the Caribbean. The submission is therefore made that our logical first step at this critical juncture in our history is to pursue a fresh appreciation and greater understanding of the radical nature of creative power.

The quest must be preceded however by an assumption that will determine all other assertions—it is the critical assumption that first we must make contact with God, for He is the source of highest rational thought and of all power. He is the One to whom all power belongs. Real power is of God!

What the world waits to see is a nation that understands 'power' differently. The different perspective I speak of is one that emphasizes the internal understanding of the concept of power rather than the external. I speak of the need for all of us to begin to appreciate 'power' for its essence rather than its trappings. I honestly believe that in this region today the need is greater than ever for this new perspective on power. We have only to examine the serious imbalances now a part of our lives—in our families, our institutions and organizations, our marketplace, our region and our world. As independent Caribbean territories, after more than 300 years of British rule, the elitist concept of power needs desperately to be changed. No longer should the political state remain perceived as an end in itself, but instead, as the means of facilitating a new end—one that is the creation of self-governing structures and processes. Such structures and processes will enable people to hold greater responsibility for organizing their economic, social and cultural affairs.

Why is this new perspective so important for us? Because, as Caribbean peoples, we have abrogated our responsibilities to 'the government'! Some governments, of course, have usurped this power, but however installed, 'governments' have become too powerful in our eyes and in our lives. Too many governments have become in effect 'all powerful.' Consequently, people have come to perceive them as all providers, meaning providers of all things. But that thinking is inherently faulty, for it sets up such perceived governments for failure since succeeding in this role is impossible of human achievement. Therefore, the State, given the task to provide all things for all men and women—a task that is physically and spiritually impossible—ends up becoming a state riddled with corruption and characterized by personality or party tyranny.

For such states, lack of integrity is all too evident. One of the important hallmarks of modern political power is its need to be visible. Thus the political directorate must go to great lengths to be seen and heard to maintain its appearance of power, and to protect its territory and prerogatives. This relentless pursuit of power becomes the raison d'être of entire governments. The latter is forced to use power to stay in power—some attempts are subtle while others are open and brash, even rash. For example, a government would use money which should be put into national programs/projects for election campaigns and/or to get the support of special interest groups. Decisions are based on political expediency rather than the real needs of the people.

This soulless pursuit of political power has led to some of the most terrifying and devastating forms of violence. Some even think that power comes from the barrel of a gun. While one may find some persons who are genuinely motivated to serve humanity and to use power creatively, for the most part, it is the 'will to power' that lures men and women to the most extraordinary and often immoral lengths in pursuit of same. Power has come to mean, the power to control lives of others, and politics have come to mean, the activity or the process to get to the position of power. This perception of power is tied up with the authority of the state which holds the instrument of force. Tragically, the state or 'government' may use this force to control citizens' lives rather than to regulate law and order and promote human justice and freedom. Political power in the Caribbean is crisis-ridden.

What shall we do? Unless as a people we wake up to what's really happening, the progress that we seek will be forever elusive. We face the danger of political power destroying us. We must, all groups within our societies—including the potentially powerfullly influential church—decide to repent of our sins as well as our failures, and seek positively to overcome our pervasive inclination to non-involvement and unconstructive condemnation. That approach, thus far, has brought us the alienation and frustration we now struggle to endure.

POWER: REDEEMED AND RECONCILED

But all is not lost. There is hope. I believe there is hope because I perceive that there is another concept of power for us to explore and embrace. This perspective is derived from the understanding that there can be a creative, reconciling and redeeming concept of power. This is a concept that emerges when power as popularly perceived is redefined and reinterpreted through Jesus Christ, the Only Begotten Son of God.

Permit me to pause so that I may clear up any possible identity confusion. The Jesus I speak of must not be confused with any other who might be so presented. Therefore, I make the further comment that I speak of the Christ who came from the eternal heavens into temporal human history, or put another way, I speak of the Lord God omnipotent who condescended to identify Himself with us "in the flesh" and so dwelt with us, even though retaining in Himself "the fullness of the Godhead bodily"(Colossians 2:9, KJV). The coming to earth of Jesus, of course, was to be our Savior. He came to redeem us all, members of spiritually fallen and lost humanity. It is in and through and by this **Jesus** that the unique concept of the 'power' I speak of is gloriously revealed, and made gloriously possible. From Jesus we can learn much about power. When Jesus acted He did not demonstrate a worldly power. When He stood before the politician Pontius Pilate, the Roman Governor, who failed to discern the difference in their perspectives, Jesus knew that Pilate was not aware of this superior concept of power, and so to enlighten the benighted Pilate, Jesus boldly told him, "My Kingdom is not of this world" (John18:36 KJV).

The world where this dynamic spiritual concept of power reigns is essentially spiritual. Yet, it is a power available to us for we are all spiritual beings. Today, this same power is available to all who are willing to believe and receive and use it. This power in the spiritual realm is available to us through Jesus Christ, the channel of God's grace and goodness. Of course, the offer to receive this power might be rejected as many are inclined to do, but not denied. The reality of this power is too evident to be denied. The availability of reconciled, redeemed power is there for all those willing to accept the existence of this dimension of power. To the aware and alert concerning this power, the possibilities are endless for a new awakening in body, soul, and society. Jesus stands ready to dispense this power to the faithful who are hungry to receive it. Jesus assures such persons that "they shall be filled" (Matthew 5:6 KJV).

This is the power that the world needs desperately. This is the power that Jesus invites all of us to embrace and so as to become transformed by its dynamism. This power does not rely on use of threats or display of force. This concept of power is creative, compassionate, reconciling and redeeming—unique indeed. This view of power is of course diametrically opposed to the existing view of worldly power, and is more about freedom than bondage; life not death; inner transformation more than outer conformation. God's power entrusted to us humans is intended for reconciliation; not revenge. Ofcourse, there are some people who are inclined to consider this kind of 'power' to be weakness. This is because it seeks not after its own but the best welfare of others. This is the 'power' best employed for restoring relationships and for promoting justice and fair play throughout society, at every level, in every place. This kind of 'power' is not about 'advancing' reputations and inflating egos. This kind of 'power' is not about seeking to ensure 'success'—'by any means possible' or by any means measurable. This is a radically different concept of power. I speak of the power that is nevertheless attainable, by God's gracious provision, through Jesus Christ. I speak of spiritual power.

Spiritual power! What's that? Spiritual power is the supernatural power that proceeds from God and is made available to all who recognize and accept God in Christ Jesus as the only source of transcending power. How can we tell when the power that we seek or use is spiritual power? It comes with a relationship with God in Christ Jesus, and *two* measures will always be of much help to make us discern this mysterious, powerful stranger in our midst: Divine *love* and sincere *humility*! This kind of *love* clothed in *humility* is that which benefits more the receiver than the sender. This kind of love is that which demands that power be used supremely for the good of others. Power put to the service of arrogance and conceit is dangerous and destructive. However, power under the discipline of humility is teachable and willing to learn from others. Creative, authentic power is both self-limiting and vulnerable. We are free to admit that we are not always right. We come to a dawning realization that the more power we have the more difficult it may be to make right decisions; the more alone we may feel about the responsibility demanded for the proper exercise of this power.

This life-giving creative power is of use to us only as we can work it out in real life in our homes, in our communities, in our governments, in our world. We can choose un-regenerated, humanized, and restrictive power that is normatively used to dominate and manipulate or we can choose creative spiritual power that is used to lead and liberate; and to make us holy and honorable citizens. Foster acknowledges that "it is only through the grace of God that we are able to take something as dangerous as power and make it creative and life-giving."[43]

SPIRITUALITY OF POWER

There are two main types of power: Godly, spiritual power, and human, worldly power. Power carries with it a "spirit". This "spirit" when divorced from godliness is demonic and evil. The spirituality of worldly power lends itself to darkness. As we consider the reality of the spirituality of power, we may wish to apply the concept to our organizations, institutions and systems. Every organization, institution, culture and society has a spirit which defines and underpins its power relationships. The closest the social scientist may come to recognizing such a phenomenon is to talk about the motivational influence which affects the structure and culture of organizations or societies. But I argue that it goes much deeper for I make the link with such causative motivation and the influence exercised by the devil in his manipulation of the world though people and institutions.

Perhaps it will be useful at this point to identify some of the sources of power in our world and the spiritual forces that underpin these systems. Donal Dorr identified four pyramids of power: *money power*—the small number of individuals, corporations, countries who have or control economic resources., *political power*—the group of people, including politicians, who control decision-making, or exert influence and authority over the directions of other people's lives, *idea power*—those who influence how people think and feel, e.g. the Media, the world of fashion, the world of education, etc., and *religious power*—those who control the beliefs, value system, ideology of others, often in the Name of God or for the supposed good of humanity. [44] All of us spend our energy and ability giving legitimacy and support to the above systems which form an integral part of our lives. We never stop to question the true source of their power. We never question the nature of their control over us and their ability to influence our values and attitudes. We seldom discern the spirituality of the power of the institutions that shape our lives.

But by our neglect to probe the spirituality of power we falter seriously, for the source determines the quality of the streams that form those head waters or headquarters. The spirituality of power is real. It is pervasive and persuasive. It possesses individuals and groups as well as systems and structures of society. There is no person and no society untouched by the insights we might bring to understanding the spirituality of power.

13

For example, political institutions, which gain their legitimacy by seeking, gaining, or obtaining, and holding power, are particularly susceptible to the control of spiritual principalities or evil power.

Let us pause to understand this—the very real principalities that manifest themselves in our societal structures and institutions account for the destructive bent often present in the seeking and securing of power politically. The evidence is all around us. None can deny the passionate pursuit of power, and not only in public office, but in our organizations, in commerce, in religion.

It is only as we begin to understand what the Bible calls "principalities and powers" (Ephesians 6:12) that we can truly begin to confront the power issue in our individual lives and in our social structures. We are entreated to examine our own self-seeking behaviour, our greedy thirst for power to rule and control, very often invoking the name of God and patriotism. Let's face it, certain secret enemies are among us and must be exposed and denounced and even destroyed. Demonic power must be opposed. Such power at work generates false pride and false patriotism. Such power deludes us into thinking that we or our party or our group or our religion is always right. This constitutes a great evil, for pride tends to brook no interference, no correction, and no criticism. Many of the world's greatest tragedies were propelled by persons, many of them politicians, who saw themselves as accountable to no one. Therefore, energized by the spirit of pride, coupled with the power to delude and deceive masses of people, they wreck havoc in the lives of millions. Hitler is a classic example. There are of course, several examples closer to home and nearer in time. One need only reflect for a moment at the contemporary scene of political leadership.

How do Caribbean people go about re-conceptualizing power for positively transforming our selves and our countries? A good beginning is for us to confess. Let us begin by identifying and confessing our shortcomings; by appreciating that we are in spiritual warfare (good versus evil). Too many of us disdain spiritual realities. When our spiritual eyes are opened we will be able to review more discerningly our realities. Look at how easy it is for us to welcome and enthrone from among ourselves a Moses or Joshua or some kind of deliverer or revolutionary leader. There is an urgent need to be more discerning. This challenge to better discern evil powers and plans is by no means easy, especially when there is dangled before us juicy carrots of prosperity and progress for every man, woman and child. But we must resist easy appeals to advance.

Greed is an evil power within and it is one of the besetting sins of fanatical power seekers. Greed uses any means to advance its selfish cause. Technology is the 'new-kid-on-the-block' in the community of greed. It is imperative that we become aware that technology like fire can be a source of blessing or disaster. Let's speak plainly and practically; the 'cell-phone' can become a god. Our political and economic systems are characterized by insatiable greed, over-excessive technology and unrestrained aggressions as well as sometimes unnecessary militarism

What must we do? Indeed, the contradictions, chaos and conflicts of the world today may leave us feeling helpless or hopeless. The choice is neither panic nor passivity. We must protest and struggle against the currents of evil and oppression everywhere. Our children and youth are being destroyed, our leaders discredited, our environment devastated and our culture is being degraded. We must fight back intelligently and include in our armory spiritual weapons. We must not simply seek out some scapegoat to crucify or imagined savior to glorify. Nor must we go the way of all flesh in offering obeisance to some system and obedience to some master. We must resist any enticement to new enslavement. Our way forward is to rise up, in the name of Jesus Christ, from our indifference and complacency and our fear and rebelliousness and cut a new path of independence, inspired to pursue a new way that leads to recognition of Jesus as our authority for every program and policy, the regenerator of a "new heart" and provider of a transformed life.

Michael Witter [45] while declaring that he was speaking from the perspective of scientific socialism based on a philosophy of materialism, makes a passionate plea for the church to go beyond the protest that comes from Liberation Theology and beyond protest against the poor conditions in which people live and begin the work of participating in the constructive building of a new society. He makes the fundamental error of not realizing that the new society is not possible without the 'new man'. It is the creation of this 'new human being' Jesus prioritized when he told the religious

Jewish leader that even religion could not save him. Jesus made it plain to Nicodemus that he had to be 'born-again' if he ever hoped to enter the Kingdom of God.

The emphasis of this appeal is for the revolutionary experience of regeneration to begin in the heart so that it can spread to the society and inform and transform the structures. The new concept of power being advocated begins necessarily with interior change. It is this new understanding of power that is needed to be worked out in moral principles to establish righteousness in political organizations and other societal structures. Rest assured that when this new understanding of spiritual rule grips our hearts then all falsity will have to be set aside. Our special interest groups will become spiritual interest groups. We will begin to make decisions not based solely on bringing benefits to ourselves. We will begin to recognize and confront the evil workings of primarily protecting vested interests and pursuing policies of self-aggrandizement. We will seek prudently to identify and destroy demonic spirits that lie behind unjust and immoral laws and oppressive social and corporate structures.

This revolution in philosophy and theology that will be felt tremendously in society will not happen overnight. That's why it should begin today. Jesus did not leave us with an organizational blueprint for its implementation but he left us with the motivation to determine its creation. The ball is now in our court to reverse the slide of history and climb toward the mountain top with fresh hope, renewed love and strengthened faith.

SPIRITUAL POWER AND CULTURAL POWER: THE CARIBBEAN HOPE

Two important and inevitable tasks face Caribbean people if we are to survive the often tribal onslaught of political power which characterizes our day and age.

Firstly, Caribbean peoples need to recognize and receive the gift of spiritual power which has its basis and finds it meaning in an infinite, personal God. Here, spiritual power is the action and influence which come from the supernatural union of God's Holy Spirit with the human spirit. It comes as a gift of God received in a personal relationship with God through *faith*. From this vantage point, power shows forth as coming from within. It displays itself as *authority* which comes from spiritual strength, not from status or position. This kind of power cannot be easily explained by rational or natural means. Indeed, it can only be understood as it is perceived to be from God and to be of God. We must as individuals and as a people become open to accept this liberating, creative power which is gifted to us humans. To share in God's power is to be fully and truly human.

Secondly, as Caribbean peoples we need to restore and revitalize our cultural power by taking stock of our history, our present situation, and our destiny from a world view which has God as the first Creator and final Arbiter of history and destiny. To leave God out results in a distorted view of the past! As we leave God out, we lose our sense of direction and destiny. As Carl Ellis correctly notes in his excellent little book, entitled, *Beyond Liberation: The Gospel of the Black American Experience,* when we fail to live our lives as God bids us, our values and attitudes, our wisdom and knowledge, indeed the whole of our collective consciousness become false, foolish and self destructive.[46]

Permit me at this point, to briefly explore the complex issue of Caribbean culture which has received considerable attention in our debates and dialogue; intellectuals and scholars, inside and outside of the region, have for decades exercised themselves as to the nature of Caribbean identity. From my reading of the views of the experts on this subject, I do agree with Neville Dawes in his preface to the late Rex Nettleford's book on *Caribbean Cultural Identity* that "Caribbean man has [indeed] arrived as a functioning totality, [and we need to decide,] objectively and with full attention to the details of our existence, what options to choose from the multiplicity offered us by history." [47]

Wendy Grenade, political scientist and university lecturer, in exploring the notion of the Caribbean cultural identity draws our attention to the work of renowned Caribbean writer, George Lamming. According to her, Lamming defines culture as the very basis of society, not just "the icing on the cake" but "the very cake you are making". Lamming is described as seeing culture in the way we define and present our selves. He uses the idea of the *sovereignty of the imagination* as the capacity we have to define ourselves and control our minds.[48]

While in some measure I can support such a bold assertion, my argument would wish to take this a step further and submit that the sovereignty of the imagination which is mandatory to Caribbean people as we choose the options afforded us by the multiplicity of our history, *needs* a transcendent source for its ultimate meaning. It cannot be an end in itself. It must find transcendence in the Sovereignty of the Godhead. Consequently, I would be inclined to say that our first task must be to recognize and acknowledge the Source of the gift of spiritual power. And then, with gladness, take the priority step, which would be to creatively use God's enabling gifts to further His agenda for promoting truth, justice and beauty within our homes , communities and world.

Interestingly, Darrow L. Miller in his insightful article entitled "Culture: Where the Physical & Spiritual Converge," talks of humankind's task as "culture makers' to reflect "the three faces of culture". In that regard, he identifies: *truth*, God's physical and metaphysical laws, *justice*, God's moral laws, and *beauty*, God' aesthetic laws. He then argues that recognition and application of all three of these fundamental laws lead to *life, health and development*.[49] In assessing his conclusive assertion, I find the above typology an intriguing and useful one since the avowed pursuit of *life, health and development*, often summarized as describing "well being," remains high on the agenda of just about all Caribbean nations. If we choose to accept his submission, which I am inclined to do, then I would be logically led in following through to believe that such end-results emanate from a culture that is based on truth, justice and beauty.

If then as nations we are to achieve the much coveted "well-being", it behoves us to apply Miller's philosophical underpinning to our Caribbean cultural realities. This of course, means that our view of life must be consistent with God's creative, spiritual power which alone can move us from our present destructive bent to increasing maturity and wholeness.

God's power, spiritual power must be used in ministering to the needs of our nations, in service to others and in pursuing well being. The use of power therefore becomes a *ministry* to others, and not a way of exercising *mastery* over others. The example of how Jesus used such spiritual power should instruct us for He entrusted the ministry of power to ordinary people—people whose lives resembled in important ways, the lives of Caribbean people today. They were poor, hardworking, and controlled by national elites and foreign rulers. Yet to this disenfranchised group of ordinary people was entrusted extraordinary power.

We can see then as we seek to learn from the Gospel narratives that the ministry of power is common property to all peoples who would seek and receive such. This is the perspective needed if we are going to become involved in working toward ensuring that the deeply religious roots of Caribbean people be transformed from mere religiosity to true spirituality, from worshipping in a manner that merely reflects a form of godliness, to worshipping in a manner that truly reflects the effectiveness of the Spirit of God, Who is *the* Source of real and authentic power.

When as a people we make the decision concerning who is ultimately in control of power and governance, then will be released a mighty force of spiritual power that will make us become increasingly free to serve. Once we make this decision from among our peoples will emerge leaders with servants' hearts, who are willing to face their citizens in honesty and with integrity, not promising easy solutions, not providing pat answers, not usurping individual and community responsibility, not compromising hard won democratic principles for easily lost political expediencies, but committed to seeking just and meaningful solutions to the difficulties and dangers of real life.

This is the vision being cast, the vision of becoming a people in possession of spiritual strength and power that will stand firm with the eye of *faith*, with the mind of wisdom and discernment, with the skill of practice and experience, with the commitment to stewardship and service. With spiritual courage and competence, we will let go of our empty posturing and procrastinations which now reflect what can best be described as vain and futile political charades. We can then shift our preoccupation with, and belief in superficial and artificial economic prescriptions and solutions—often imposed from outside and bent on control of people and resources—to the more sustainable, far-reaching and indeed exceedingly painful and prolonged process of empowering people through a Spirit-directed sharing of power.

By such conceptions and exhibitions of power, the voice of spiritual authority, will then call our people to responsible and creative living reflected in our life goals and life styles. With the wisdom of God, and through the grace of Jesus Christ, we will look for concrete and realistic solutions to the problems of a region which though small in size is yet richly blessed with natural resources which can provide a life of simplicity and quality for most, if not all.

The foregoing agenda speaks indeed of the ministry of power. Such a ministry will work to reconcile, liberate and unite Caribbean people who today more than ever need a restoration of our relationships. The need for such transforming application of power could not be greater for our history has demeaned and divided us. Our economics has made us more competitive than constructive and more crippled than creative; while our politics has left us more alienated than animated, and more apathetic than alert.

This vision for a new way of seeing and applying power needs to be the particular focus of our current leaders. The need for this appeal is urgent as we have played a defective role for so long outside of the ministry of power, that our vision has become blurred, our actions non-productive and largely futile; motivations are cynical and hope severely dimmed. We find ourselves wandering in a spiritual and cultural wilderness marked by frenetic and feverish activity at one extreme, and by unconcerned and irresponsible apathy at the other end. Both produce the same result: No real change.

Clearly, our problem is lack of meaningful vision. What we may claim as Vision is at best continuation of the status quo with the logical consequence of no real change. We must develop and use our spiritual power to re-create a new vision of cultural power based on responsible freedom and creative unity. As the Bible sternly warns, "where there is no vision a people perish (Proverbs 29:18, KJV).

So what kind of Vision is needed? We need a vision based on a concept of spiritual power expressed socially and culturally in policies, programs and projects involving the following three dimensions, (1) reconstruction of our history, (2) realistically reviewing our present situation, and (3) recapturing our destiny.

The *first,* reconstructing our history, will require us to see things from God's point of view. We must get back to the authentic, though often painful, aspects of our history. Much of what has been written about us has been sifted and selected by people other than ourselves or persons whose frame of reference has been shaped and formed by those same others. It is heartening to note however that more and more Caribbean historians are rewriting our stories. Our children and youth need to read and critique those new and different perceptions about ourselves and to use them creatively for dealing with the present times.

The *second* task of realistically reviewing our present reality will be largely dependent, of course, on what we do when we attempt to recreate and rewrite our history. When we attempt to do that we will have to necessarily have a God-centered view of the world in order to have an adequate understanding of our past. The prevalent world view on which much of our history is based provides only a two-dimensional view of the world. It is a limited reality - even a distorted reality and so causes us to truly misunderstand who we are and whence we have come.

The *third,* the recapturing of our destiny, is a problem we are consequently landed with for we have become unclear about our destiny having been so misguided as to our God-centered beginning and purpose. Not surprisingly then, many of us have forgotten where we are going. Others, especially our young people have never known about meaningful purpose for in general our lives have been externally directed. Therefore, in seeking to find answers that will enable us to recapture our destiny, we will be forced to return to our roots, to the authentic aspects of our Caribbean culture.

But the task will not be easy, for cynics abound to question the validity of the premise concerning what is proposed in this book—a return to God, as biblically revealed. Consequently, there will be many who will question aggressively and perhaps dismiss arrogantly whether there is such a culture. Our wanderings in the wilderness for centuries leave us restless and rootless.

Therefore, spiritual warfare must be waged in a battle for the mind and hearts of our Caribbean people, in order to find meaningful answers. This will necessarily involve careful re-interpretation of our history and our perceived destiny which are now limited to our present two-dimensional view of life. This search must include an expanded dimension—a third dimension that says in effect that God alone is able to give meaning to that additional reality and guide us through the flow of history toward our true destiny.

In pursuit of casting a desirable vision, we can take from Darrow L. Miller's reminder that as God-created "culture makers" it matters hugely what kind of culture we create. Consistent with this, we can say that a true appreciation and understanding of our culture will lead us to see that it is a reflection of all that we believe in—a manifestation of our faith, our world view. "Culture," Miller says, "stands at the convergence of the spiritual and physical realms . . . ; the spiritual realm influences the physical realm at the level of culture".[50]

Miller helps us to see usefully that culture is not neutral. He helps us to understand that we can indeed critique our culture distinguishing between those things that promote corrupt practices or just actions, economic greed or economic well-being; between a *counterfeit culture* which leads to impoverishment and enslavement, and *a kingdom culture* which leads to freedom, justice and truth.

In the review and re-examination of where we are as a people today—we are moved to a renewal of our collective consciousness. This collective consciousness involves our standards, values and attitudes; what we do and how we do it; the framework that we use to understand our world. It is only as we begin to see the world as God sees it, will our values and attitudes provide a true reflection of our present and our future. As long as our world view remains distorted, our values will continue to deteriorate and degenerate into the inevitable path of falseness and self-destruction. The socio-political and socio-economic experiences and realities of the region today reflect this falseness and self-destruction. We must pursue cultural power based on a clear acceptance of the power of God to renew, revitalize and redeem our history, destiny and consciousness.

Many of the Caribbean's brightest have rejected the idea of God, wrongly concluding that it is a part of our historical baggage—that it is western imagery and symbolism foisted upon us by our colonizers. Many accept the scandal of *'the God delusion'* [51] In our attempts to free ourselves of cultural symbols that we believe to be not our own, we have left out those aspects that we cannot see, analyze and explain. Therein, we have made the fatal mistake: much of our analysis omits the reality of the unseen—the supernatural. It has inevitably led to godlessness and as Carl E. Ellis points out, Godlessness leads *to a* kind of cultural death.[52] We have already seen clear demonstrations of this not only in our region but in the world. The need to place God centrally in this act of reclaiming cultural power is offered without apology, though humbly. Until as humans, we recognize that our very personhood takes on transcendence from an all transcendent God, until we accept that all of reality cannot be explained by natural means, until we can bring the two realities together—the natural and the supernatural; until we can come up with a meaningful synthesis of the spiritual and the natural/physical, all our analysis, conclusions, prescriptions, all our social economic and political engineering will be incomplete, imbalanced and vain.

As we are hurtled along by the startlingly dramatic changes taking place all around us, the tendency for some of us is to become mesmerized and hypnotized by those things that we can neither understand nor accept; others of us are moved into panicky action in an attempt to save ourselves from being sucked under by the rising tide of global events. The time is right to harness the strength, inventiveness and creativity of Caribbean people with a view to working out imaginative and workable alternatives. The option proposed in the foregoing discourse may seem theoretical, to some even impractical. True, it remains merely theoretical only because it is largely untried. But the fact that it is untried hardly means it is impractical. The reality is that our traditional ways of viewing problems and doing politics, sharing power and building culture have not only proved to be impractical but having been obviously and consistently tried, have been found wanting. It is tragically unwise to fail to consider changing the rules of the game when the game is clearly killing us. We are experiencing cultural death.

As we move swiftly into the twenty-first century and face what sometimes appear to be insurmountable global challenges, we need large portions of wisdom and grace, love and discipline, courage and humility, peace and community to work out a vision of cultural power within the ministry of spiritual power. There is no room for retreat; there is no time for procrastination. There is no chance like now to dream, to plan, to work and to hope. This is the responsibility to which we are called as Caribbean leaders and citizens.

Myles Munroe, contemporary Christian theologian, gifted Caribbean writer and internationally renowned speaker throws out the challenge, especially to Caribbean people, for the urgent need to move into what he calls, the ***Age of Responsibility***. According to him, for too long we have wandered around in the wilderness seeking easy manna, refusing to accept the freedom, the real freedom, to which God has so graciously called His human creation. He asserts boldly: "Freedom demands responsibility."[53] We are called from the position of having others do things for us and to a posture of moving forth resolutely to our destiny as a region. He urgently reiterates the need to shoulder the real burden of freedom as, "There is no greater burden than freedom, no heavier load than liberty"[54] The choice is ours. What will it be for us as Caribbean peoples? Will it be *responsible freedom* or *irresponsible enslavement*?

PART II

RE-CREATING STRUCTURES:

A PROPOSAL FOR CARIBBEAN SURVIVAL

THE CONSTRUCTING OF A VISION OF CHANGE

"Where there is no vision, a people perish"
Proverbs 29.18 KJV

Having briefly explored two models of political power, one as humanized and compromised, and the other, redeemed and reconciled, the latter of the two models which constitutes spiritual power, is offered as an authentic source of hope for the Caribbean region. This view of power is of course based on a theistic or biblical worldview which recognizes the Sovereign God of the Universe as the Source of all power—being omnipotent, omnipresent and omniscient. God is Spirit and from Him proceeds, all benevolent spiritual power. Therefore, my submission is that a vision of change for twenty-first century Caribbean must have as its basis *spiritual power*.

Perhaps it will be useful at this point to reiterate the definitions or more accurately descriptions used in this text to define *spiritual power*. Power is defined in the *Concise Oxford Dictionary* as "the ability to do or act." I would add, the ability to influence for good or ill, positively or negatively. Spiritual power when mentioned is the supernatural power that proceeds from God and is made available to the human who sees and accepts God as the Source of all transcendent power. It is creative and life-giving. Richard Foster succinctly states, "It is freedom not bondage . . . transformation not coercion . . . that creates and restores relationship and gives the gift of wholeness to all!"[55]

Creative power is redemptive power. It is using one's influence to heal, reconcile and restore relationships. It is refusing to use one's political clout to benefit one's self or one's significant others. It was the power used by William Wilberforce (1759-1833) who spent some of the most productive years of his life advocating for the abolishing of the slave trade. It was the power used by Nelson Mandela, despite his immense suffering, in leading in the process of ridding his beloved country of the awful scourge of apartheid. It was the influence used by Mother Theresa in fighting to protect the hungry and homeless children of Calcutta. It is the power which comes from ordinary women and men who are able to forgive unspeakable harm done to them and their loved ones. Spiritual power is at work all around us if only we can discern it. Alas, it is tragically missing in the halls and assemblies that are alluded to as "seats of power" of our nation states. Creative Spiritual power sets people free and sometimes it may look like weakness and that's the precise point where it is truly redeemed and reconciled. It is the kind of power that the Caribbean needs to see more of reflected in humble servant leadership. Too few of our leaders display the humility and integrity of redeemed and reconciled power. How we long for some more of the ilk of Grenada's Prime Minister Tillman Thomas! I wish to submit that it is only redeemed and reconciled power that will give effectiveness and life to a vision of change for our region.

As I move on in my discourse to the urgent task of constructing a vision of change based on the strength of spiritual power, I propose the re-creating of structures which are underpinned by a biblical worldview and which results in authentic spiritual and cultural power as the only hope for the region. Cultural power here denotes the strength and solidarity of a people as they define who they are and what they are becoming. It is the spiritual resistance exerted by a people as they move against forces and barriers that would in any way demean them as full and free human beings made in the image and likeness of God.

This *re-creating of structures* is not structural adjustment of the 'right' nor structural 'transformation' as propounded by the 'left;' it is a re-generation of our structures, bringing new life to bear, impacting with new life the institutions and systems which contribute to human well-being, based on the power of the Supreme Creator and Sustainer of the Universe Who from the very beginning made His world "good". This vision of change that I seek to offer is characterized by what John Stott describes as "a deep dissatisfaction with what is and a clear grasp of what could be. It begins with indignation over the status quo and grows into an earnest quest for an alternative".[56]

The discussion in the following pages commences with an exploration of the traditional paradigms of *structural adjustment* and *structural 'transformation'* as advanced by the conservative secularists (capitalist perspective) and the revolutionary secularist (socialist perspective) respectively. The argument is advanced that both traditional paradigms have a secular-humanistic, materialistic base. Built on the sand of humanistic power, they do not have within themselves the ability to bring about authentic and sustainable change. Both paradigms have indeed propounded prescriptions and strategies that have left the region disunited and undeveloped, with little cultural power to exert the spiritual resistance needed to move increasingly to social and political well-being.

The bold proposal for Caribbean survival is what is described as a "fundamental paradigm of human transformation," informed by a biblical world view, built on the rock of spiritual power and resulting in structural re-creation. In this vision of change, three major tasks confront the region: developing economic self-reliance, building political community and transforming social relationships. All three are briefly explored, concepts defined and some prescriptions offered as a platform for ongoing reflection, analysis and action.

A DIRGE TO DREAMS—THE TRADITIONAL PARADIGMS

All around us dreams are being shattered! Precious hopes are dimmed . . . changes are taking place so rapidly . . . voices rise shrilly and hysterically asking for real answers. Many lose faith and succumb to the seeming lack of meaning and purpose. Several lose hope and see no future. Our young people are especially hard hit.

I wrote the above paragraph in May 1991, almost nineteen years ago. As I re-read it today I see how aptly it describes the scenario which faces our world at this time of writing.

I would like to quote from an article entitled, "Reflections on the Global Economic Crisis" by Darrow L. Miller renowned speaker and writer on Christian apologetics, and social and development issues:

> If you are like me, you are wondering what is going on with the economy. This is certainly the worst financial crisis we have witnessed in our lifetimes, and yet it may reach or exceed the severity of what has been known as the Great Depression of

the 1930's. On a personal level, I have watched my life savings diminish by about 35% in the last year, and there seems to be no end in sight. Credit is hard to come by. Food and gas prices have soared. People are losing their houses and their jobs. While this is certainly impacting the poor and the middle class in the industrialized world, it is perhaps a greater crisis for the poor in the least developed world. The rise of food and fuel prices in these countries is devastating.[57]

Miller noted that people were anxiously looking for answers and scapegoats, identifying policies of the Bush administration, policies of Congress against the banking system, greed on Wall Streets and CEOs of major corporations, "futures traders" in Dubai, Freddie Mae and Fannie Mae and anyone else they could identify.[58]

On Sunday, May 03, 2009, I listened with real interest to Dr. A. R. Bernard, Senior Pastor of Christian Cultural Center, Brooklyn, New York, as he commented on the present global economic crisis to thousands in his congregation, *"the crisis of the world is not an economic crisis. It is a **crisis in character** that has resulted in this economic chaos".[59]* (emphasis mine). He underscored the fact that the crisis of the world was a moral one based on sinful moral choices and would require much more than economic solutions. Closer to home the Minister of Finance of Grenada in a Television interview in January 2009, sombrely predicted that the unemployment rate in his island state could rise to 30% by year end. In late February, 2009, a Member of Parliament and Minister in the Cabinet of the Government of Barbados, to a large crowd of expectant party supporters of the ruling Party, the National Democratic Congress, painstakingly and powerfully portrayed the gloominess of the economic prospects for the Caribbean as a result of the global economic crisis, and called on the crowd to understand the times and be patient with their government.

Sir Dwight Venner, Governor of the Eastern Caribbean Central Bank, on Tuesday, March 03, 2009, at the launch of a public consultation process on the establishment of the OECS Economic Union, made a strong and reasoned case for the integration of several small Eastern Caribbean countries. He pointed out the tremendous challenges and the series of external shocks faced by our region—fuel, food, finance—and underscored our critical domestic challenges, among them being, underperforming private sectors, weak civil societies, alienated youth, crime and violence, and extreme dependence on government. He articulated a vision of a space of peace and tranquillity where *"new forms of government and governance"* would emerge, and where *"vibrant, flexible and adaptable economic arrangements would develop"*[60] Much of his hope is pined on economic integration of the region beginning with the Eastern Caribbean countries. He sees the critical challenges facing our region, both externally and internally, as demanding deliberate and swift action for our very survival.

Everywhere in the Caribbean Region, from North to South, East to West, the refrain remains the same. We are in trouble along with the rest of the world. The "storm signals" predicted for the Caribbean way back in the early nineties are now exploding on us with full, gale force winds, pulling down insurance companies, threatening banks, exposing risky investments and downright fraudulent deals, and leaving a trail of unemployment, underemployment, disappearance of hard earned savings and vulnerability of once safe mortgages and loans.

The Commonwealth Caribbean Region of just over four million people is undoubtedly part of the global human maelstrom of escalating fear and madness. As a region, our smallness in size has always been said to work against us. I wish to contend however as I look somewhat sketchily at the economic, political and moral constructs of our life and society, that our smallness may, in fact, be the critical factor which will contribute to our continued survival. Caribbean people have grappled long and hard to find meaningful solutions to the politico-economic problems of the region. We move between the weary rhetoric of structural "transformation" and the almost brutal pragmatism of structural adjustment. In the process, our people become confused by the contending and often contradictory viewpoints. Our youth become embittered and totally disillusioned. Some shout anarchy; others would welcome tyranny, if only it promises some semblance of sanity. The energy and motivation of our brightest people are sapped and eroded, and a spirit of disinterest, selfishness and hedonism holds sway.

Is there any way out of this morass of clashing ideas, self-centered motives and counter-productive action? Do we settle for the death of our dreams, a burial of our hopes, and the extinction of a people? The burden of this discourse is to explore some of the factors responsible for our present position, and to begin an attempt at offering some possible alternatives—ideas which, for me, are still gestating and which would require much discussion, debate, dialogue and critique by, and with those who would wish to join in the search for new options. No doubt, I'm a late-comer in this search and feel sure that there is much to learn from those who have already taken the risk of challenging the status quo.

A brief examination of two of the traditional paradigms which have provided the economic/social framework of our present modus operandi will be attempted in order to demonstrate the faultiness of our basic assumptions and the weakness of our essential premises. The main traditional paradigms which have guided the political economy of the major part of our world are based on either the Capitalist or Socialist/Marxist mode of thought. Capitalist neo-classical economic theory in seeking to address the many problems/contradictions facing the several ailing economies which fail to proceed along prescribed development paths have posited the concept of structural adjustment, today re-casted under the name of the Poverty Reduction and Growth Facility (PRGF). The vehement socialist critique of Western Capitalism on the other hand, will stop at nothing less than structural transformation. One seeks to tinker with the system, the latter to tear down the system. What is significant about both positions is that though the means may be different, the ends/goals are the same—world progress through ever-increasing technological growth. But even more germane to this discussion is the fact that both positions share a mechanical view of the world—a view that leaves little room for real transformation and lasting change—a view that leaves out the transcendent and spiritual—a view that leads indeed to a dirge for our dreams.

I wish to spend sometime looking at the concept of *Structural Adjustment*, since for us in the Caribbean this prescription carries with it the painful cry of distress and the bitter ring of defeat. Caribbean economies are based on conventional neo-classical theories of economics. The policy measures which sought to deal with the problems facing developing countries were concerned with the management of structural change and the development of feasible combinations of market forces and government intervention.

Notwithstanding increasing growth rates in many developing countries, a high level of disequilibrium persists. This takes the form of wide-spread unemployment, low productivity levels, strong dependence on export of a few primary products, massive importation of goods leading to a preponderance of distributive trading, heavy reliance on foreign investment and aid, low levels of domestic savings and so on. The picture remains one of uneven, imbalanced development, with the rich growing richer and stronger, and the poor (who make up the majority) becoming increasingly marginalized and powerless.

Recognizing disequilibrium as an observable feature of many developing countries, a new policy agenda was sought. The traditional monetary/financial institutions like the World Bank and International Monetary Fund supported and adopted policy measures to avoid disequilibrium with a view to achieving more rapid development. These measures were characterized as adjustment mechanisms. Today, a number of third world countries, including several in the Caribbean, find themselves plagued by a life threatening debt crisis, exacerbated by a critical shortage of foreign exchange to keep their import-oriented economies afloat. Peggy Antrobus, in very early days, noted that the price of the assistance received from the International Monetary Fund to deal with these crises, was a package of policies known as *structural adjustment*. She pointed out that this particular policy mix included cuts in government expenditures for health, education and social security, as well as for utilities, including low income housing, the imposition of charges on basic services and the devaluations of currency.[61] Maxine Henry-Wilson in commenting also on the structural adjustment package pointed out that this intervention was aimed at equilibrium and stability, "using the market as the mediating mechanism".· the State was to assume a 'hands-off policy' while the private sector plays a 'get-on-with-it' role. This is to allow the market to function freely and competitively. The expectation is that the consumer will be sovereign; products will respond to sovereignty; prices and other costs will find their mark by the free play of all forces of supply and demand. [62] It seems to me that one very, very important variable was left out of the scientific equation—*human greed*.

Joan M. Purcell

Events in the world, at the time of this writing have shown how faulty are our assumptions. What actually takes place is a far cry from the stated presuppositions. The assumptions are faulty, the consequences are disastrous, with few exceptions. The economy moves into ever increasing dissonance, and dependency is further entrenched. The dream of economic take-off turns into an ever present nightmare of going under! For us in the Caribbean, the story is familiar. The fear is real. The future is bleak unless we can change our present course. A number of strongly argued reasons have been put forward to account for the extremely precarious position in which many Caribbean countries now find themselves. Whatever the propositions offered for the limited success or lack of success of structural adjustment policies, which were meant to correct imbalances and which appeared to have only deepened imbalances, an alarmingly dangerous situation was exposed and documented on the negative impact of these measures on women, especially poor women and by extension their families and communities. Women are the ones who suffer most from cut back in social services, imposition of wage freezes, and the removal of price control. The devastating impact on the economies of Guyana and Jamaica following structural adjustment programmes left little room for debate. The very measures which were intended to offer salvation to the poor, vulnerable economies appeared, instead, to spell economic disaster and led these countries closer and closer to national genocide.

To sum up, three basic principles guide the economic model of our region: the determination to advance through economic growth; the commitment to use ever higher technology; and the practice of making trade more and more international. These commitments of course lead to a number of problems, namely, resources are used up more rapidly than they can be replaced, giving rise to undue competition; more and more people are unemployed; nations become less and less self-sufficient as they depend more and more on imports (Grenada's import bill as of December 2008 stood at EC $ 985 million, with fuel import alone being $69 million, and export totalling only EC$90 million—Ministry of Finance, Grenada 2009); countries are forced to borrow increasing amounts to meet the basic needs of their people, thus becoming trapped by heavy debts. It has recently been estimated that fourteen (14) out of the thirty (30) most heavily indebted countries of the world are found in the Caribbean[63]

The vicious cycle continues when one is forced to concentrate on paying debts rather than using the already limited resources for the development of the country, in order to get more loans, as is the case in Grenada today. A substantial amount of Grenada's annual revenue goes toward repayment of its unprecedented debt of EC$1.7 billion.[64] There is urgent need to challenge the economic idols of growth, technology and progress and to re-examine the underlying assumptions of these goals, which appear to be working against us rather than for us. In the late seventies to early eighties, a number of our Caribbean political economists alarmed by what they viewed as the permanent crisis of capitalism and its disastrous consequences on third world economies, including the Caribbean, and the failed attempts of the socialist experiments in Guyana and Jamaica, sought to elucidate a vision for Caribbean survival. Beckford and Witter noted that the solution of the International Monetary Fund (IMF) locked the Jamaican economy tighter in the prison of the international capitalist system.

The writers restated their commitment to a proposal for change based on a socialist transformation of structures of society. They were convinced that the basic condition for a socialist path of self-reliant development is a transformation of the political and social environment to release the creative dynamic of the disposed masses of Afro-Jamaican people. For them the goal of the "political economy of transformation" is to produce "integral man", which involves "pulling together the pieces of an alienated man . . . into a coherently articulated integral man and society."[65] They contended that the basis for this transformation of man and society lies in the resolution of the class struggle. People are to be awakened to their true condition, their consciousness raised to oppression, and the oppressive forces and structures surrounding them which are spelt out chiefly in economic terms within a capitalist/imperialist framework. The struggle between opposing forces must ensue. Once eyes are open people will actively work together for what will undoubtedly be in their own interest.[66] Then, as summarized by Elaine Storkey in her exploration and critique of the socialist agenda, *"Class identities will be solidified, new demands made and the tight control which capitalism exerts over all our lives will start to move."*[67]

35

Just as the capitalist explanations and expectations of the workings of free and competitive market forces are incomplete and often contradictory, so too the socialist transformation process (greatly simplified as described above), though important in significant aspects of its analysis, carries fundamental weaknesses within its framework. The socialist critique focuses almost solely on the economic in order to explain complex human behaviour and human structures. I wish to submit, however, that a lot of what is wrong with our society is not necessarily dictated by the structure of the economy, nor the nature of its politics, for that matter, but is more likely to be a problem with the structure of human relationships and the worldview which drives these relationships and systems. This central problematic is not adequately resolved within the socialist transformational model. The belief that massive economic and political reconstruction alone can save us, leading to the emergence of a new socialist developmental agenda has not been borne out by history, especially contemporary history.

Both models of economic development—be it capitalist or socialist—carry an unwavering faith in human rationality and human nature. One places enormous responsibility on equal individuals functioning in a free and competitive market to act rationally and fairly for the benefit of all; the other looks to a particular class or group to act collectively and ideologically in order to achieve economic transformation and political liberation. Both models, as already stated, are predicated on a mechanical view of life; both are working from the enlightenment perspective of the inherent ability of men and women to solve their own problems. This deep seated commitment to the innate goodness of the human being makes both positions over-optimistic regarding the possibilities for transformation and change. Neither an adjustment to the structures of market and government, nor a change in the system of production allocation is enough to resolve the basic issues of real human greed, corruption and selfishness. At the centre of the human heart is **real sin** (not all sin of course). Neither a tinkering with the system nor a tearing down of the system speaks concretely to the central problem. These humanist perspectives, though necessary, are definitely not sufficient. The challenge is to find an alternative option which offers more convincing answers to the complex question of the human condition. To this I now turn my attention.

A SONG OF VICTORY: THE FUNDAMENTAL PARADIGM: HUMAN TRANSFORMATION

Caribbean people have been challenged by two main propositions—adjustment of our structures verses transformation of our structures, reflecting a capitalist or socialist agenda respectively. Neither has delivered the goods, though some may argue that the socialist agenda of Cuba, notwithstanding its cost in human freedom, has been a success story in many ways. The experiences of several African States on the other hand are quite instructive. Whatever the real or perceived outcomes of the particular models, it is my view that the debate needs to be lifted out of the above stated polarizations. Neither structural adjustment nor structural transformation per se can breathe new life into a people nor recreate a society. These forms are essentially external and rational. The deeply internal and spiritual dynamism remains largely untouched while the predominantly external imposition of new forms results in no <u>real</u> transformation of the lives of individuals or of the life of the society.

The structural responses that have been examined in the proceeding discussion objectify our economic problems in ways that at best are only partial and at worst wrongly based. Both positions offer help in analyzing and understanding economic issues, yet because they start from the view of human autonomy, both fall into trap of making the problem total. The root of the debate goes back to the way one views life—one's **world view.** It has been pointed out that much contemporary social science is based on the Enlightenment and as the late Francis Schaeffer observes, "The utopian dream of the Enlightenment . . . was thoroughly secular in its thinking . . . here was man starting from himself absolutely . . . ; to the Enlightenment thinkers, man and society were perfectible."[68]

The Enlightenment was described as a movement directed by a **new faith.** Its first basic belief was that man was the shaper of his own destiny, had rights and freedom, and was subject to no higher authority. Man became autonomous! The then prevailing acceptance of the basic sinfulness or depravity of man as articulated in the Judeo-Christian tradition was replaced by a belief in the natural goodness of the human race. Elaine Storkey offers this characterization, "Nature was venerated, bringing an emphasis on natural law, natural justice, natural theology, natural rights and undergirding it all, the natural right of reason."[69] Enlightenment thinkers moved the basis of belief in God away from revelation, to nature and reason with huge implications.

The economic models under discussion, as said before, are part of the same basic tree whose roots go back to Enlightenment. It is this very foundation which is ultimately responsible for their failure to come to grips with some of the basic problems of our society. Having thrown out the concept of a Personal, Infinite God who is maker and creator of history, and who is knowable, they have laid claim to the belief that human life is independent of God and His revelation, and that the socio-political struggles of a people transcended the religious and spiritual.

Leaving God out has significant consequences. Our social scientists' perspective of the world becomes distorted. Yet all insist that their reality is the ultimate, often presenting their limited perspective as the whole truth. Today our world is locked in a battle of opposing viewpoints, with each side offering prescriptions which are believed to reflect the best characterization of reality; notwithstanding the fact that globally, we are experiencing tremendous dislocation and disorder; nation states are in constant conflict and upheaval, and individuals are increasingly depersonalized and dehumanized. Our attempted human autonomy constitutes the very heart of the problem. We therefore need to turn from the rationalism and secularism of the Enlightenment and find a firmer base for our fight for solutions—one which has a much more realistic understanding of what it is to be human.

I wish to submit that a more truly comprehensive and overarching paradigm is propounded within the **worldview** which begins with a Personal, Infinite God, Who created the universe and **ALL** its elements and resources, made man and woman in His own image and likeness, gave them **freedom** to live in open communication with Him, to love, to produce, and to be stewards over the earth's resources. In space time history, man and woman became separated from God through an acted-out desire to control their own lives, thereby moving out of the Creator/creature relationship, into a self-willed, self-centered life style. The Infinite, Creator God immediately set in motion a plan to redeem and heal this tragic rift.

God chose to speak to humankind propositionally, revealed truth through His written word—the Bible, and even more importantly through His Son, Jesus Christ, who broke forth into human history, living in space and time, revealing the very heart of God to humankind and making the way to bring back fallen human into a right relationship with God. God continues today through the power of the Holy Spirit to transform and empower the heart of individual humans to live a moment-by-moment, day-to-day relationship with Him, based on **grace** and **faith**. Such a transformed life seeks to honor God and to bring healing, wholeness, affirmation and love to others, and the structures and institutions which form our human society.

This plan of God touches **all** of God's created order, both human and non human, and will find its ultimate fulfilment only in **HIM**, through **HIM**, by **HIM** for all times and all ages. Man's repeated attempts, therefore, to displace the God of the Universe can only end in futility and tragedy. We humans have built and continue to build models, ideologies and theories based on our own limitedness and finiteness. The base is insufficient, the foundation is weak. When pressures come—economic, political, and social—everything collapses at our finite feet. This is what is happening so dramatically today to our structures and systems. They are burdened by the weight of human engineering. They fall under the fragility and frailty of their own finitude.

All of the social sciences have dealt with the issue of human transformation in one way or the other. This indicates an almost universal recognition that the possibility for change in the human is real and that the necessity for change is critical. Theories differ on how these changes take place. Most see it as an educational process, where people gain increased knowledge of self, others and the world around; develop critical consciousness and experience perspective transformation, learn new and appropriate behavior patterns and act out rational choices for the benefit of self and society. Research has indicated, however, the difficulty encountered in attitudinal change vis-à-vis behavioral change. It underscores the point that internal change is not the same as external conformity and that real change from the inside out is always difficult. No theory has yet been able to completely or satisfactorily explain the complexity and diversity of human motivation and behavior—the reason why some people, in the same situation, change and others do not, why even in the best ordered environment people will act contradictorily? What constitutes the nature of human love as well as human deception and depravity? And what triggers the lust for power in some and the enormous human sacrifice made by others? The apparent paradoxes remain a part of the mystery of human life. What is quite clear is that human nature is multifaceted and complex; simplistic definitions fail to capture its richness, diversity, perversity and capriciousness. The human is one and the same time is wonderfully noble (being made to mirror God's image) and essentially flawed and depraved (having rejected our oneness with God). The human heart is splintered being separated from God, and our minds divided, being bent on thinking our own thoughts apart from God. It stands to reason therefore that only a Personal, Infinite God (The Creator) can do the work of integrating finite, personal beings (His creatures). The human dilemma is basically a spiritual dilemma and can only be truly resolved in the light of a correct analysis and understanding of the nature of the problem.

I wish to begin with the foundational premise that **man and woman** are made in God's image. We are both flesh and spirit. We experience bodily physical birth in our first encounter with the external world as a result of the physical union of our parents. The second imperative is spiritual birth or regeneration. This comes about through the union of God's spirit with our spirit. Jesus' authoritative statement that "ye must be born again" was preceded by His explanation that "that which is born of the flesh is flesh, and that which is born of the spirit is spirit" (John 3:5-6 KJV). The human heart is made for communion with God and remains fragmented, restless and full of a nameless yearning until this mystical, supernatural union takes place at the will of God and the willingness of the human. It is unashamedly simple, yet profoundly spiritual in essence. Each individual is called to a deeply personal, transformational relationship with God in Jesus Christ. This spiritual transformation begins with an attitude of "childlikeness"—a sense of wonder and humility, characterized by the recognition of a finite creature standing naked and unashamed before an Infinite Creator who encompasses all of life, meaning, purpose, truth, power and love.

Most of us humans live our lives trying to exist outside the circle in which God made us to exist. We try to be what we are not, and, indeed, as a consequence, all the elements of what we are as humans rise up against us. We experience true moral guilt. It is only as we come to the recognition of this moral guilt, and with simple, conscious, childlike faith accept our creatureliness and confess our moral guilt before a moral God, can we begin the transformational journey to healing and wholeness. This journey is for many gradual and uneven and for others sudden and dramatic, but for all, is marked with depths of pain and petition, as well as flights of ecstasy and praise.

God begins His transformation process in the hearts and minds of the individual woman and man. This process does not, however, stand alone. We are sent, indeed mandated, as agents of change, as disciples, both as "prophets" and 'lovers," to work out our faith with fear and trembling—not with arrogance and pride, never pretending a perfection that is simply not possible for finite humans. We are to be "salt" and "light." We are to influence the transformation of structures and institutions of society, **not with the intent of making them into the kingdom of God**, but with the aim of bringing them more closely to a reflection of values inherent in God's Kingdom—values of truth, integrity, courage, compassion, based on principles of love, justice, peace and freedom. We are warned against the dangers of utopianism and perfectionism. Although God offers in *this* life substantial healing of our relationships, our institutions and structures as we choose to go His way, we do well to accept the transitional nature of our world—a world which is tragically marred and which must await its ultimate deliverance by God through Jesus Christ, and not through human engineering.

As finite human beings seeking a correct understanding of God's plan and purpose for this universe, we will, with a mixture of sadness and hope, accept the imperfect nature of God's creation, while it waits expectantly for the day of its redemption. This process of change can never be fully explained. Lawrence Crabb cautions that neither must we expect precision in our understanding of spiritual change, nor should we display over confidence that we are saying all that needs to be said—the work of God's Spirit cannot be neatly packaged into predetermined categories,[70] [a dangerous tendency of humanistic theories and models].

Having begun this journey with a spirit of childlikeness portrayed in Jesus' own words *"unless you change and become like little children you will never enter the kingdom of heaven"* (Matt.18:3, NIV), one continues in the WAY with a spirit of Christlikeness. This spirit is characterized by love, joy, peace, patience, kindness, goodness, faithfulness, gentleness and self-control (Gal.5:22NIV). One recognizes immediately that these characteristics are diametrically opposed to the world's norms of selfishness, greed, discord, deceit, envy, disloyalty, immorality, warring and slothfulness. Only the spirit of a Holy God can save humankind from its downward bent to deterioration and destruction. The need for hearts which are transformed and minds which are renewed by the touch of God's spirit are critically and urgently needed as we face a possible collapse of civilization.

In conclusion, I wish to draw on Donald Dorr's commentary on a balanced spirituality, which, for me, sums up so well **a spirituality of transformation**. It is based on a verse of Scripture from the Book of Micah. One of the Minor Prophets of the Old Testament:

> *He has showed you, O man what is Good.*
> *And what does the Lord require of you?*
> *To act justly, and to love mercy, and to walk humbly*
> *With your God (.6:8, NIV)*

The Lord's requirements of man involves firstly, a "religious conversion" which is primarily an awareness of who we are before a Sovereign God, and acting upon this awareness, the willingness to enter into a living, experiential, liberating relationship with God through Jesus Christ empowered by the Holy Spirit—walking humbly with God. Secondly, the Lord's requirement speaks to a "moral conversion" which includes the healing of our interpersonal relationships and our commitment to love—to love tenderly and mercifully—ourselves and others for God's sake. Thirdly, we are called to a "political conversion" (to act justly) where we are to be found working to build a society that is intrinsically just—a society in which the structures are just.[71]

I wish to subscribe that human transformation must be rooted in all three conversions in order to make any deeply and lastingly significant impact on the work for a more humane and just world order, including, of course our economic and political systems. Without the latter experiences of transformation, our models are nothing more than clashing, clanging cymbals; our assumptions are based on the transiency of shifting sand, and the greatest tragedy of all, the consequences of years and centuries of applied social theory which are death-producing rather than life-affirming.

Let us turn now to examine some options aimed at re-creating our structures; these options are by no means original and must never be seen as ends in themselves. They are meant to provide the framework of an alternative paradigm, based on the sobering reality of our universal human condition and a realistic assessment of the physical and socio-cultural resources of the Caribbean Region.

A PRAYER OF HOPE—AN ALTERNATIVE PARADIGM: STRUCTURAL RE-CREATION

Hope is the feeling that what is desired is possible of attainment . . . hope . . . comes from shattering false illusions and replacing them with new truths.

Jeremy Rifkin

The time has come for some new answers to old questions. It is clear that our world cannot survive on its present trend. It is also clear that it requires a certain boldness tempered by gentleness, a lot of courage balanced with humility, and a real vision shaped by eternity to move our existing generation from its self-destructive course of either escalating despair or consuming complacency. Jeremy Rifkin offers a challenging critique of the prevailing mechanical world view as he examines the basic assumptions of world progress through the lenses of the Entropy Law. He sees the world as becoming increasingly disordered, being run on a view of life that is inherently incorrect. According to him the classic economic theories cannot solve the growing crises facing the world's economies. According to him, both socialist and capitalist nations model their economic assumptions along the lines of the classical mechanical doctrine:

> Capitalist economists continue to view the economic system as a mechanical process in which supply and demand functions are continually readjusted to each other in forward and backward motion . . . while socialist economists reject the market mechanism, they agree with the capitalist economist that the overall economic environment is never depleted. [72]

Rifkin contends that both schools of thought assume that with increasing technology new resources will always be found. In essence they view the resource base as inexhaustible.[73] According to the theories, economic activity turns waste into value. All that is needed is to add human labour to create surplus, and this, of course, may go on indefinitely. Rifkin reminds us, however, that the first law of thermodynamics expressly states that all matter and energy is fixed; it cannot be created nor destroyed—only its form can change, never its essence. The second law of Entropy Law states that it can only be changed in one direction, from available to unavailable, usable to unusable. These two natural laws carry enormous implications for our present trend in technological development, and our view of economic progress.[74]

Whether Rifkin's entropic theory is accepted or not (I personally have found it both intellectually and practically compelling) it points to an essential economic challenge, namely our stewardship of the earth's resources. It also provokes us to re-examine the basic assumptions of a world view where power and progress are defined by and derived from our ability to exploit and own the world's resources, and questions our preparedness to make peace with our earth and with each other.

In attempting to offer an alternative paradigm, I have come up with the theme "structural re-creation." I am minded not to present a position that throws out of the window all of our lived stories and experiences which are central elements of our social institutions. My intent is to call forth values and principles which will undergird these institutions and such as will emphasize our humanity as well as our divinity—God created man in His own image and likeness (Gen.1:27 KJV). Further, I wish to emphasize that the thoughts expressed in these pages are not original with me—most have been borrowed from a number of writers whose propositions and reflections have found a strong echo in my own heart as I search for new life-affirming ways of seeing, believing and acting. In recreating structures, we will be attempting to breathe new life into our economic and political systems based on the notion that human beings, against all the forces of nature (the law of entropy) continue to evolve, and as we evolve as individuals *"we carry humanity on our backs."* [75] As the miracle of evolution takes place in us humans (and I refer more specifically to our spiritual evolution) our institutions and systems must come to reflect more of that which we are.

I turn now to a discussion on developing economic self-reliance, building political community and transforming social relationships as the key tasks of structural re-creation. An economic system articulating a theory, to borrow a slowly popularized phrase, "as if people mattered," must, from this perspective, be based on the concept of self-reliance underpinned by the principles of stewardship and simplicity. It emphasizes our responsibility to take care of our God-given resources, our obligation to meet the real needs of our people, and our endeavour to match our resources to our needs with a view to produce results which reflect the best possible combination of equity and efficiency. To put it another way, a model of economic self-reliance based on the principles of stewardship and simplicity is offered as a proposal toward re-creating our economic structures. Self-reliance here is not intended to mean absolute independence nor total self-sufficiency. It is propounded more as a re-creation and regeneration of structures/systems through one's own effort, capabilities and resources. Johan Galtung articulates a clear commitment to economic self-reliance as an important alternative to conventional economic thinking—the concept of self-reliance is the antithesis of much of the thinking behind the growth economy; *"the primacy of the market in conventional theory must be replaced by the addition of other mechanisms for the satisfaction of basic human needs. The second task of an economics of self-reliance must be to find ways of producing what is needed, through reliance on ourselves, on our own production factors, meaning, nature . . . labour . . . capital . . . research and administration."* [76]

Based on the theory of comparative advantage, a division of labour takes place between economies—usually a developed and developing economy, or to put it another way, the centre and the periphery respectively. So Grenada exports cocoa and nutmeg to North America and Europe to be refined and returned as imports. North America provides aid which comes with special conditionalities often more beneficial to the donor than the recipient. One must buy British trucks with British aid or Venezuelan oil with Venezuelan loans. A country must be a source of cheap labour in order to attract much needed investment capital and technology, a nation must accept Casino Gambling in order to get external investment, and so on. The inequities and imbalances between centre and periphery are reinforced and perpetuated.

The economics of self-reliance seeks to reduce and replace the <u>use</u> of one economy by another as an external sector for "dumping negative externalities" while denying that economy the experience of producing "positive externalities".[77] Galtung clarifies his position as follows: "*. . . the basic rule of self-reliance is this: produce what you need using your own resources, internalizing the challenges this involves, growing with the challenges, neither giving the most challenging tasks (positive externalities) to somebody else on whom you become dependent, nor exporting negative externalities to somebody else to whom you do damage and who may become dependent on you.*"[78] An economics of self-reliance, notwithstanding its emphasis on looking to oneself to meet one's needs and solve one's problems, recognizes that there is often a gap between what is needed and what can be produced on the local level.

This brings us to the purpose of exchange and trade and introduces the concept of regional/international/global <u>interdependence</u>. Economic self-reliance does not purport to replace trade and exchange. Such trading must, however, be guided by equity on the terms of trade and the development of a country's potential for self-sufficiency in basic needs such as food, clothing, shelter, etc. The economics of self-reliance, however, cannot be perceived in purely economic terms but needs to be sustained by the recognition of ethical/moral dimensions to international/regional relationships. Denis Goulet, a strong proponent of this view, criticizes traditional economic and social development theories because of their emphasis on materialism while they ignored the qualitative aspect of life and proposes the common values of life sustenance, esteem and freedom as indices of development in all societies.[79]

Galtung equally supports value-based development and views self-reliance as *"psycho-politics"* as *"it presupposes and builds self respect"*.[80] It changes the way in which people are enabled to perceive their own potentials and capabilities. In order to be firmly rooted, the economics of self-reliance must begin in the community, move to the nation, spread to the region and then unto global interdependence. Self-reliance must result in a collective character—developing into *"a process of interdependence among equal partners as a means for solidarity to prevail over blind competition."*[81]

For Caribbean people, the concept of community is an extremely important one. Maxine Henry-Wilson proposes that the market model of economics be replaced by that of the community. She posited:

> The concept behind the paradigm which places the community as the focal institution of socio-economic and political development relates to the need to redefine power and to see these relations as mutual, complementary, and transformative . . . the two-person model of the market is replaced with interactions governed by shared values. Commodities do not become end in themselves but means to achieve ends. These are the prevailing ethos that regulates community life. The economic relationships emphasize a match between need and resource ability . . . . The evolution of a paradigm which uses the community as an institutional framework also ensures that there are larger social systems and institutions which regulate and influence behaviors and ensure social control . . . reduce remoteness and alienation,... give people control of their environments and hence make them more empowered.[82]

Though the potential of Caribbean communities has remained largely untapped, our historical experiences demonstrate that our people, when motivated and mobilized can rise to the toughest challenges. Our present economic model continues to foster dependency; having sapped the energy and creativity of the majority of our people it has left our small countries divided and fragmented. The choices are clear to many of us: continued strangulation and stagnation by the "ole economics" or a bold, new start in search of self-reliance. Which is it to be?

I wish to propose to those who are courageous, two fundamental principles which must inform our search: <u>Stewardship</u> and <u>Simplicity.</u> Stewardship is a biblical concept; it relates to the management of our God-given resources. Francis Schaeffer points out that human beings are given the responsibility by God to act as stewards over *His* creation—to protect, preserve, develop and use for the good of humankind and the Glory of God.[83]

Rifkin sees the newly emerging stewardship doctrine—one that's diametrically opposed to the theory of "dominion"—meaning to manipulate and exploit—as a fundamental critique of the modern world view which includes centralization of power, technological excesses to meet consumer demands, fragmentation of labour, devastation of the environment in the name of progress and other such goals.[84] He said further:

> Stewardship requires that humankind respect and conserve the natural workings of God's order. The natural order works on the principles of diversity, interdependence, and decentralization. Maintenance replaces engineering . . . the new steward-ship doctrine represents a fundamental shift in humanity's frame of reference. It establishes a new set of governing principles for how human beings should behave and act in the world.[85]

The concept of stewardship says that people do matter. It says that people are infinitely more than matter. We are central to God's design of the world and anything—even if it is seen as progress—which pushes people aside, which replaces people with machines has to be anti-human. An economic model where people matter, which incorporates the outworking of the stewardship covenant means "adopting living patterns that make us partners of nature rather than its exploiters".[86] It also means that we would explore and utilize sources of renewable energy such as solar, wind, water, biomass, etc., while we seek, as much as possible, to conserve our non-renewable sources of energy. Our focus would be on appropriate technology rather than utilizing the latest technology at all costs regardless of its impact on the earth and its people. The profit motive will not be the only criteria for selection of technology; instead, careful thought will go into assessing its impact on the level and nature of employment, energy path, and environmental factors. For example, the Caribbean Region may find that it needs to redefine its TOURISM to make it more compatible with its natural habitat and cultural heritage.

The perception that agriculture is hard, dirty, unrewarding work mainly for old people, will have to be replaced by the view that our land is, for many of us, our richest natural resource, involving hard work, yes, dirty work, often, but the means by which we grow our food, build our houses, and keep our families and communities going. We may need to look into the real benefits women derive from export-processing zones (jobs yes, but the type of employment and the quality of work are also critical issues that require our attention). We must begin to take a hard look at the proliferating calculators and word-spellers which, as efficient as they may be, could spell disaster for the mental development of our children and youth. We may wish to question the wisdom of our huge expensive satellite dishes and our cable networks which bring into our hearts and homes a portrayal of life that is often superficial, shoddy and deliberately shocking. We may need to examine our present enslavement to the 'cell phone' which robs us of the ability to communicate face-to-face and which siphons off millions of dollars from poor economies to trans-national corporations who lead us to believe that we cannot exist without them. The myth that the higher the technology, the greater the progress and development, must be exposed, and its real costs, especially to further generations of people, must be thoroughly calculated.

You may wonder at this point what type of living I am advocating. Am I supporting a life style that is uncivilized and uncultured? Am I against science and technology? To these questions I will return a strong negative. The type of living proposed in this alternative economic model is found in a life style where <u>people</u> must matter—all people, not just a few, not just a race nor a class. The God who has made us, made sure that none be left out, "*For God so <u>loved the world</u> that He gave His Only, Begotten Son that <u>whosoever</u>* believes . . . (John 3:16KJV). We humans, however, are left with the challenge, responsibility and privilege to share the earth's resources justly and equitably. Moreover, we can do a much better job, if more of us were prepared to live simply.

Simplicity is another biblical principle. "Simplicity sets us free to receive the provision of God as a gift that is not ours to keep and can be freely shared with other.", so says Richard Foster[87] who, at the same time, throws out a strong challenge to those of us who seek alternative models:

> "Courageously we need to articulate new, more human ways to live. We should take exception to the modern psychosis that defines people by how much they can produce or what they earn. We should experiment with bold new alternatives to the present death-giving systems. The . . . discipline of simplicity is not a lost dream but a recurrent vision through history. It can be recaptured today. It must be.[88]

The principle of simplicity espoused here neither refers to personal mortification nor a renouncing of possessions. It is, rather, referring to a style of living that would allow more and more people to have a reasonable, fulfilled life and to share in the earth's resources. A model of economic simplicity will focus on reorienting our economic goals so that the accumulation of possessions would not be judged as criteria for success or as an indicator of development. This principle challenges vested interests in an affluent life-style. It challenges a model of development that appeals to rugged individualism, greed and envy; it means "changing the modern patterns of production, distribution and consumption, by the promotion of a more simple and frugal way of life."[89]

Donald Dorr offers six compelling reasons in support of a life-style of simplicity:

a. to ensure that the poor has a fair share of the limited resources of the earth;
b. to preserve and protect our environment;
c. to promote bodily health;
d. to reduce the stress of modern living;
e. to assist in the provision of full employment and satisfying work;
f. to provide the opportunity for the development of an educational system that is neither unrealistic nor alienating.[90]

Such a model stresses the elimination of unnecessary accumulation and waste, the promotion of usefulness and durability of possessions, a compassionate sharing of wealth and resources, the elimination of exploitative and oppressive relations and practices, the development of greater personal fulfilment and individual tranquillity, a rediscovery of the marvels and wonders of nature and a thankful appreciation of God's creation. The model would of course be lopsided and sentimental if it did not encourage the recognition of the dark and cruel side of nature and the tragic and destructive propensities in us humans. A life style of simplicity is not a retreat from the realities of life; rather it is an attempt to discover or rediscover what real life means with its beauty and its ugliness, its blessings and its banes.

Some proponents of a simple life style envisage broad and sweeping structural changes resulting in a "civilization of simplicity" where meeting the needs of the "masses" is paramount. Others see it more as an inward reality that results in an outward life-style; both of these realities are missing from contemporary culture whose most destructive feature is "an insane attachment to things."[91]

The principle of simplicity implies and promotes a breaking away from the prevailing economic/cultural ethos, which perhaps can best be done by small pioneering groups whose task will be to share a vision of a life that is not wasteful and cluttered with unnecessary possessions. At the beginning of this discourse, I made the point that our smallness in size may in fact work to our advantage. Relatively small countries, with fairly homogeneous and cohesive communities may have a decided advantage in leading the way in positive experiments with alternative life styles which can have immediate impact on the wider community. Of course, we know that attitudinal and behavioral changes do not occur overnight. Moreover, people will adopt only that which appears to offer benefits to them with the minimum of risks. The challenge will be to make real this vision to our Caribbean people.

An economic model that stresses simplicity will never produce waste and over consumption and will result in greater equity for our people and increased self-sufficiency for our nations—goals which we dare not ignore if we are to survive. The principles of simplicity and stewardship within the context of self-reliance offer a direct challenge to nearly every economic value of our contemporary society based as they are on un-regenerated materialism and unrestrained technological progress. Our modern economic system, moreover, has taken root notwithstanding its contradictions and convolutions. It has enveloped our institutions and systems and has captivated the hearts and minds of our people. Any direct challenge to these entrenched values will meet with substantial scepticism and resistance. Undoubtedly, it will involve a process of change. A process for which we may not have too much time and which will involve not only economic structures and choices but also political goals and aspirations.

I wish to submit that any movement to economic self-reliance has its best chances for success through the building of political community. The Lausanne Covenant (1974) defined politics as "the art of living in community."[92] I rather like this definition. It lifts politics above the realm of gross manipulation, raw expediency and ugly intrigue (where it now appears to be firmly anchored) and places it in the arena of dealing with creative tension, human paradoxes, and conflicting interests and demands. In this arena problem solving and conflict resolution are means to consensus building and community strengthening. Living in community is by no means easy. As a political act, it involves the sharing of power and therefore carries with it far-reaching, often life-threatening impact especially on the non-material aspect of life. Yet for all its obvious difficulty, there is a great deal of truth in Scott Peck's categorical statement that, "In and through community lies the salvation of the world. "[93]

Community as a concept is used rather loosely and has different meanings for different people. I wish to continue with Scott Peck's elaboration of the concept of community; according to him, it is "inherently mysterious, miraculous, and unfathomable."[94]

Therefore to capture its essence in a single definition is inadequate. He sees the seeds of community as residing in humanity and, like gems, community becomes possible through "a process of cutting and polishing".[95]

Real community though difficult to describe, does carry certain intrinsic characteristics. Peck identifies three: inclusivity, commitment and consensus.[96] If community is to be real, it must be willing to extend itself and to struggle with the widespread phenomenon of exclusivity. It must be aware of and appreciative the full range of human differences and human experiences and be prepared to celebrate them.

This of course requires commitment to work together regardless of individual differences. It involves a willingness to coexist and a preparedness to stick together when things are tough.

The same transcendence that takes place at the individual level must take place in the community as people's attitudes toward each other change—alienation is transformed into appreciation and reconciliation. The politics of this change can hardly be accommodated within our modern version of mystified totalitarianism or watered-down democracy. Neither can provide the transcendence of differences, because both leave out a substantial group of people from the process of change. Genuine community seeks wide consensus. A difficult task! Some would say an impossible goal; others, however, describe it as a challenging adventure which is strangely mystical, but which works when put to work. Real community, for all its magic, is essentially based on realism. Its inclusion of a variety of points of view and the freedom to express them moves a group into closer consensus. I am again moved to quote Scott Peck as he describes community: "incorporating the dark and the light, the sacred and the profane, the sorrow and the joy, the glory and the mud, its conclusions are well rounded . . . with so many frames of reference, it approaches reality more and more closely."[97]

Having participated as a Member of the Regional Constituent Assembly on Windward Island Political Unification in 1991, I was privileged to be both participant and observer of such an exciting process. For me, the process was infinitely more precious than the content (as important as that was) and regardless of the outcome of that dialogue, which was often confrontational, the people of the Windward Islands were for a short while specially touched by a sense of community and consensus building. It is my prayer that the attempts today to bring together the nation states of the Eastern Caribbean will be strongly lauded and widely supported with a "political conversion" taking place especially in those who see themselves having the most to lose. Caribbean people must with courage and faithfulness take hold of a vision of political community, or go under in a veil of national insularity.

In articulating a vision of political community, I wish to emphasize two important goals: <u>Participation</u> and <u>Peacemaking</u>. Community is integrative and participative. It brings people of all sexes, ages, religions and lifestyles into a whole without creating a bland average. The concept of the melting pot has never been realized and never will. Human beings are created along the order of both unity and diversity and no ideological or cultural goal can change that. A process of community, as said before, encourages distinctiveness, and furthermore involves the growth of participation—people's participation. Almost all of our governments give assent to this notion. This is, in large part, due to the fact that community participation is essentially a political process. It involves sharing of power and, if really pursued, means a reduction of power differences between government and governed. The dark side of politics, including Caribbean politics, has not welcomed a diminution of power. The result of this hoarding of power has been the continuation of dependency and infantilism among our people. These characteristics are antithetical to the growth of self-reliance and self-confidence. It contributes to a tragic wastage of our human resource and enormous un-productivity of our already limited material resource base.

We must be prepared to go the difficult, though definitely more rewarding route of people participating in their own development, beginning at the level of their local village/community, and moving out into the wider regional/global community. It is not my intention to go into details of strategies and approaches to community participation. This is an area which has received extensive documentation. Furthermore, within our Region, some important experiments have taken place and continue to take place; many of these facilitated by non-governmental organizations. Governments and political parties will do well to learn from these experiences. I wish to reiterate, however, that community participation harnesses the creative capability and often hard-won experiences of people, with their diversity of rich insights and traditions. It mobilizes the community to act supportively and constructively rather than resistively and defensively. The process of participation results in building of community skills, competencies and consensus.

One of the often recognized barriers to people's participation is the fact that it is time—consuming. It is a slow process which must take its pace from the people who have often been debarred from information, knowledge and power. The movement from a sense of powerlessness and being planned for, to a critical, participative involvement is a transforming, educative, often threatening process. The time consuming nature of this process undoubtedly contributes to its cost. When one views, however, the failure of so many of our expensive development efforts, where people were not involved, then the issue of cost needs to be reassessed. I wish to note also, the often frustrating nature of people's participation. Powerless people frequently internalize dependency and inferiority described in the literature as "learned inefficacy". Their own social reality is negated and despised. The government or the expert has all the answers. This attitude must be recognized and worked around. Indeed, participation holds psychological and social costs and may be refused by those who need to be involved. Notwithstanding the costliness, time-consuming and frustrating nature of people's participation, it is my contention that its real contribution to human development far outweighs the obstacles to be encountered in instituting such a process. As we continue to pay lip service to people's participation, we contribute to the wastage and dehumanization of our richest and, for most of us in the region, our only resource—**our people.**

Although the process of community making involves the accommodation of a great deal of chaos and conflict especially in its initial stages and throughout critical periods of growth and movement, the building of political community involves on its agenda the important goal of **peace-making**. It is the view of many that violence has reached its highest stage in the present world system. The late Professor Madan Handa, Lecturer in Peace Education at the Ontario Institute for Studies in Education was convinced that we were experiencing the highest form of violent social structure.[98] We are now able to destroy ourselves with the touch of a button. Peace is therefore seen as a basic condition for the survival of humankind. The danger of annihilation is ever present because of the weapons of mass destruction that science and technology have placed in the hands of human. Peace is also the indispensable condition for economic and social development. Wars divert energies and resources from the improvement of conditions of life. Mass poverty, growing unemployment and increasing inequalities of income and opportunity undermines its basis. Peace is also a necessary condition for the fulfillment of human community: we are divided between race, class, age, gender, religion and national lines to name just a few. We need peace to direct our energies and resources to the promise of real community. One may well ask how do you deal with the elusive issue of peace? Is peace possible? Is it too late? Can we turn the tide around? To live without hope, is the end of life, and so long as there is life the search for peace remains a paramount task.

I think it is extremely important at this point to interject that though the focus of this present discussion is on socio-political peace, an immensely significant and absolutely critical pre-requisite to the latter state, is the need for personal and inner peace. I agree with Joshua Liebman that

> Social peace can never be permanently achieved so long as individuals engage in civil war with themselves . . . a co-operative world can never be fashioned by men and women who are corroded by the acids of inner hate . . . and the much heralded "society of security" will remain an utopian vision so long as the individuals composing that society are desperately insecure not only economically, but emotionally and spiritually.[99]

In my discussion of human transformation, the point is underscored that peace on the individual level comes from God, and peace on the collective level is underpinned and maintained by a dependence on the Sovereign God. We are, however, admonished in the Scriptures to plant seeds of peace. We are blessed for being peace-makers. My concern is, how can we do this in the market-place of our lives?

In addressing the latter concern, I wish to elaborate briefly on the nature and content of peace-making. I will seek to do so within a process that is herein referred to as peace education or education for peace. Peace education is, for me, learning to live for one's God, with one's self and others, and with all nature. A tall though not impossible order!

Johan Galtung in discussing peace education identified four values which he thought provided an acceptable formulation for peace, namely absence of violence, economic welfare, social justice and ecological balance [to these I would add spiritual maturity][100] The erosion of these values, he felt summed up the world's major problems. Peace education for Galtung necessitates dealing with the major forms of dominance in the world. He does not however see the challenge emanating from those who have most to lose—the major world powers. For him, true-peace education is more likely to come from among "the suppressed . . . periphery" where the real structure of the world is often more clearly seen.[101] Can we in the Caribbean, with violence being a part of both our past and present, with a long and rich spiritual heritage, and an innate sense of community, lead the way to more meaningful peace making? What a tremendous challenge!

In looking at content, peace education is not so much a subject to be taught, but is in fact a learning process which involves people in conscious, interactional, dialogue with themselves, with others and with the world. Permit me to submit three specific areas which form important elements in a process of education for peace; these are not, of course exhaustive and by no means mutually exclusive: (i) Education in peace values (values such as unity, vulnerability, integrity, harmony and hope) must become an integral part of our educational process. (ii) Education in non-violent political action (a number of innovative methods have been attempted and quite a lot has been documented on the successful use of this approach). (iii) Education as spiritual transformation, as articulated in the previous section. The methodology of an education for peace remains largely unclear. What is clear, however, is that it should begin with the very young, involving at the same time youth and adults within the formal system and utilizing other non-formal and informal approaches. This of course is a massive undertaking, and will perhaps be well served if attempted in small experimental ways. Whatever the goals, nature, content and methodology, peacemaking remains one of the most important processes and challenges for today's generation.

An alternative agenda would be incomplete if it did not include the critically important issue of gender relations and its impact on development. Lisa Ostergaard, former member of the Danish Parliament, who presided over the World Conference of the UN Decade for Women in 1980, noted that "the need to incorporate gender awareness into development efforts was recognized . . . when planners began to realize that expecting a country to develop towards modernization with the female half of its population unable to take full part in the process was like asking someone to work with one arm and leg behind their back. *"102* Ostergaard elaborates:

> Gender refers to the qualitative and interdependent character of women's and men's positions in society. Gender relations are constituted in terms of the relations of power and dominance that structure the life chances of women and men. The gender divisions are not fixed biology, but constitute an aspect of the wider social division of labour and this, in turn, is rooted in the conditions and productions and reproductions and reinforced by the cultural, religious and ideological systems prevailing in a society.[103]

The Women in Development movement, whether it is supported or not, drew to the attention of the world the fact that women, who make up the majority of the world's population, represent powerful human resources in development, much of which go unrecognized. And indeed, women's contribution to society is often clothed in the most dehumanizing and oppressive conditions. The concept of Women in Development, inevitably gave way to the broader notion of Gender in Development as the viewpoint shifted from seeing the problem as that of *women* to that of *men and women*, and more specifically the *relations* between men and women. Moreover policy makers and planners in the field of development came to the somewhat slow conclusion that what was needed was a balanced gender-aware approach in seeking to bring about any meaningful and sustainable development. Feminist theory has propounded that men have exercised *patriarchal power* over all aspects of women's lives, including reproduction, education and employment. Patriarchy, defined as *the rule of elder males of younger men, women and children,* has been widely blamed as responsible for the inequities and injustices meted out to women on a global level. The dismantling of patriarchy in all its forms has been the central goal of the feminist agenda.

Several theories on the factors responsible for the creation of patriarchy have been well documented—these include biological, psychological, anthropological and economic. A factor which the writer finds most compelling is offered by Caribbean writer, Errol Miller, when he concludes that patriarchy is learned behaviour, passed down by fathers and mothers since antiquity, [underpinned by three macro-factors] demographic, environmental and technological.[104] Miller posits that "essentially patriarchy is the exercise of power in life-taking, and matriarchy is the exercise of power in life-preserving . . . the exercise of power toward different ends . . . . the exercise of patriarchal power in society has always commanded more respect and attention".[105] He sees "women's subordination as an unintended and unforeseen consequence".[106]

Peggy Antrobus in commenting on the issue of women and employment in the Caribbean notes,

> There is no officially declared policy for the suppression of women . . . quite the contrary; official policy, even the most discriminatory type, is usually couched in terms which show a 'concern' for women and even a recognition of the importance of their contribution to society . . . . prejudice and discrimination against women is 'seldom with deliberate and malicious intent'. Existing practices are, in fact, the result of deeply ingrained attitudes of which the holders are often unconscious.[107]

Thus the real challenge is the changing and transforming of these deeply held attitudes, values and learnt behaviour. Contemporary society has seen a definite shift in the power relations between men and women, women and men. Errol Miller records that "a fundamental change" has taken place "in women's historical marginalization in societies previously organized along patriarchal lines." Furthermore these changes have had "profound implications for the psyche and mentality of men and women."[108] I wish to submit however that as fundamental as the change has been, it is not enough. The increasing liberation of women has not brought about a concomitant liberation of men. The dismantling of patriarchy simply leaves room for a new power arrangement, 'a new kind of nonsense'. As Miller elegantly puts it, "while there would be a major change in the cast, the script would remain the same."[109] I also wish to contend that in-spite of the loud and urgent calls of women, in-spite of our just and timely cause, unless men are liberated, women will never be truly liberated. Our humanist agenda though significant is not sufficient. Men and women are not simply human beings but are human beings made in the image and likeness of an Infinite and Personal God. Indeed women and men are primarily spiritual beings. And any agenda for the liberation of the human must receive its basis from the Maker and Creator of the human.

The Creator God of the universe is a relational God, Who relates to humankind in relationship and Who holds a relentless commitment to transform the relationships among His created order. God has so ordained it that the liberation of woman and man is inextricably tied together. Permit me at this point to explore three biblical themes which under-pin this submission. In Genesis, the first book of the Judeo-Christian Scripture, the Lord God of the Universe sets out very clearly the foundational premise of human relationship:

> "God spoke:" Let us make human beings in our image, make them reflecting our nature, so that they can be responsible for the fish in the sea, the birds in the air, the cattle, and yes Earth itself . . . God created human beings ; He created them godlike, reflecting God's nature. He created them **male** and **female.** God blessed them: Prosper! Reproduce! Fill Earth! Take Charge! Be responsible . . ." (emphasis mine) (Genesis 1: 26—29a MSG.)

From the readings of scripture, the creation of man and woman embodies three distinct features: equality, diversity and unity. Man and woman are made equal, sharing distinctiveness from the animals and sharing together in the image of God. Woman and man are made different, complementing each other's sexuality with different reproduction functions—the act of procreation. Man and Woman, Woman and man are made to be together, united as "*one flesh*" in marriage (Genesis 2:24KJV) and together as the two halves of mankind, providing companionship/friendship for each other and engaged in stewardship of the earth on a broader and more general level. God, the Creator, intended man and woman to live in loving relationship, reflecting the relationship of the community of the Godhead, Father, Son and Holy Spirit! Scripture, however, graphically and tragically captures the theme of spoiled relationships. Woman and man disobeyed God. Man and woman sinned against God. The result is reflected in Genesis, chapter 3, which gives a painful recital of man's progressive move away from God.

One reads of doubt, pride, greed, disobedience, dissemblance, refusal to take responsibility for one's action, guilt, shame and embarrassment, culminating with the most terrible of all: separation from God. "*So (God) drove out the man*"(Genesis 3:24a AMP). Sin, separation from God, had dramatically altered the relationship between woman and man—there was no longer innocence, openness and equality. The woman became vulnerable, the man became dominant. Human relations on a whole became tragically distorted.

The above aberrant situation is that to which the women's movement has reacted. And although we may not all agree with its analysis of the source or cause of the problem—patriarchy (male dominance), we cannot fail to recognize that there *is* a problem between man and woman. Something is tragically wrong. The imbalance is too obvious, the oppression too glaring, the failures too painful. Alas it took a secular movement to bring this situation to the forefront, but then the Sovereign God acts in the strangest of ways and uses the most unexpected and unlikely agents to do His work. The Judeo Christian Scripture, the Bible, is full of such examples. But the story is not yet finished. Indeed, it is far from over. There is a song of Redemption—a message of hope—how beautiful that sounds! This message is saying, "sin has spoiled the relationship of woman and man but has not ended it. The image is marred but not destroyed. Humankind is alienated but not abandoned." God came! God came in Jesus Christ with a message of hope and liberation, with the means of salvation and healing. Jesus came to heal and restore—to liberate men as well as women—to restore the proper balance of equality, diversity and unity.

The implications of Christian redemption for women and men are spelled out in Galatians 3: 28: "In Christ's family there can be no division into . . . slave and free, male and female. Among us you are all equal. That is, we are all in a common relationship with Jesus Christ" (MSG.). This oneness referred to is, of course, a process. It is something that we work out "in fear and trembling," empowered by the Spirit of God and the Spirit of Jesus. The transformation of relationships between women and men will not take place overnight, nor is it expected to make us the same; it will however, bring new freedom to men and women, to be **one** in Christ Jesus. Indeed Jesus began the process; He ushered in a new and dynamic set of relationships based on love and acceptance. Jesus' dealings with women should bring singing hope to women and salutary rebuke to men. Jesus never upheld the male establishment. In His attitude toward and dealings with women, He made them feel respected, loved and accepted. The story of Jesus and the woman of Samaria is well known. A multiple divorcee, half-caste and village outcast was the first to whom Jesus openly revealed his identity as Messiah. The story of the woman taken in adultery is no less dramatic. Jesus forced the men (her accusers) to be real and honest. Jesus was undaunted by the scandal caused by the prostitute who washed His feet with tears and wiped them with her hair. He forgave her! He commended the sister who was interested in listening and learning, rather than the one who was so busy and concerned with traditional duties. After Jesus' resurrection, it was women who were the first witnesses, and who were sent to share the news of the resurrection with the men who disbelieved. Jesus never condescended to women nor ignored them. Jesus' message was meant for men and women, women and men. As Christ, the Son of God, He was representative to the whole human race—He came as Human not as man—to speak to the needs of man and woman, to denounce with harshness if necessary anything that created distortion, inequity and injustice.

Women as well as men need liberation—liberation from unbelief, from doubt, from fear, from unfaithfulness to God and to each other. Men and women need to accept God's forgiveness in Jesus Christ. Forgiven woman and men are then freed to pursue love, joy, peace, patience, gentleness, kindness, goodness, faithfulness and self-control in relationships with each other. God in Christ Jesus offers us an alternative, a true and lasting and sustainable alternative!

In summary, the search for new alternatives must involve economic structures as well as political systems. A most important element of this search is to find ways to make our small size work for us, rather than against us. At the same time, regional integration must continue as an important priority. Our goal for transformation involves a self-reliant people, committed to stewardship and simplicity, and involved in the building of peaceful and participatory community at increasingly widening levels. Real transformation of our structures would, at most points, be preceded by spiritual transformation of individuals and at other times move in conjunction with our ongoing openness to spiritual health and wholeness. Our platform for truth must be firmly based on a proper Creator/Creature relationship. The inadequacy of rationalism, humanism and secularism must be recognized, and the primacy and intimacy of the Godhead embraced.

The choices facing the Caribbean people are diminishing at a frightening rate. For those of us who feel the responsibility to work for authentic and sustainable change, we are obliged to do all that we can to convince the sceptics, the complacent and the disillusioned about the possibility of real human transformation and the opportunity for substantial re-creation of our structures. We are not in this task alone: "For we know that the whole of creation groaneth and travaileth in pain . . . and not only they, but ourselves, waiting for adoption, to wit, the redemption . . . (to be) . . . delivered from the bondage of corruption into glorious liberty of the children of God" (Rom:8:22, 23,21KJV).

PART III

TOWARD A MODEL OF WHOLISTIC CHANGE

THE CHARACTER OF A VISION OF CHANGE

Vision is not dreaming the impossible dream, but dreaming the most possible dream

George Barna

In the foregoing section, three major tasks for the re-creation of structures for the survival of Caribbean societies were briefly articulated, namely: developing economic self-reliance, building political community, and transforming social relationships. What follows is a continued exploration of these and other concepts in the outworking of a Vision of change. This elaboration seeks to practicalise some of the concepts already introduced and begins to answer the vexing questions of *how* do we work out this vision. The proposed model examines four types of change: psycho-spiritual, religio-cultural, socio-economic and socio-political, focusing on the individual, the community, the market place and the society.

The character of the Vision lies in its wholistic nature and the importance of working in concentric circles, each level feeding into the other on an ever widening scale. The intent is to create a new reality that improves upon that which exists today. In significant ways it represents a response to the need identified for new arrangements in relationship and community, new forms of governance and leadership, and new visions of power and culture—a new spirituality of change. I have wrestled long and hard with linking the personal with the societal, and the local community with the national marketplace. How do you bring together all of these contending values and ideals in ways that honour our human personhood and at the same time fulfil our corporate identity as a people? The models proposed are those which have come from others who, I believe, have wrestled equally with tenacity and integrity in providing some guideposts and road maps for a journey fraught with both danger and delight. The models proposed are those which have resonated with me the most and which I have incorporated into my own worldview to provide the beginning of some strategic and practical answers to the questions posed in part one of this book, "How do Caribbean people go about re-conceptualizing power for positively transforming our selves and our country?" And, "What must we do?" All four models are consistent with a biblical worldview.

Permit me to spend some time examining the idea of "models." Harvie M. Conn comments on the fact that the scientific world was galvanized when Thomas Kuhn introduced the ideas of models and paradigms in his book *The Structure of Scientific Revolutions*.[110] Conn provided a description of models as the way we see things. He went on the note that data is perceived in terms of the combination of models—those taught and those self-constructed. Through models reality is scaled down so that we can understand it—the model becomes a paradigm. They become our spectacles, our testing ground for understanding our world.[111] I wish to submit that our existing models of change at the individual, community and societal levels are not working for our well-being. Our children are constantly at risk, home is no longer a 'safe' place; our youth are disillusioned and discontented—the jails are jammed packed with younger and younger criminals. Our communities are lacking in neighbourliness, no longer places of caring and sharing. Our cities are overcrowded and now constitute environmental hazards. Our parliaments lack civility; our cabinets lack integrity and confidentiality. Our regional and international summits lack morality—we spend millions as we come together to discuss world hunger and soaring crime rates. We build stadia costing triple million of dollars while the poor of the surrounding community has no decent bathroom facilities.

So how do we change? My answer lies in a change of our worldview. Our worldview is the control box of the culture—any change in the worldview begins a concurrent change in the culture. The Caribbean prides itself as a region of "Christian" nations. There is an urgent need to re-examine the lens from which we view our world and plan our course. Will we be prepared to change our course when we discover that our models of change are not solely constructed from biblical data but are a hodgepodge of materialism/secularism and animism with some theism thrown in for good measure? I'm reminded of the highlight of our parliamentary process—our budget debates—when our presentations are richly sprinkled with biblical exhortations while we blatantly insult and disrespect each other and attempt to deceive the wider public.

The biblical worldview, which propounds a Personal, Infinite and Sovereign God Who is in control of history, Who is the Maker and Creator of humankind and Who has a perfect plan of redemption for His

Universe, remains largely untested. While as a region we have focused on the gospel of individual salvation; we have dismissed the gospel of national discipleship and transformation. Jesus Christ in His closing words to His followers some two thousand years ago, delivered a clear mandate: "... *Go and make disciples of all* **nations**, *baptizing them in the name of the Father and of the Son and of the Holy Spirit, and teaching them to obey everything I have commanded you. And surely I am with you always to the very end of the age*"[emphasis mine].(Matthew 28:19-20 NIV),. How far short of this mandate we have fallen. The world of Christianity has spent centuries debating and in some instances concretizing a divide between the body and the spirit, the secular and the sacred, evangelism (saving of souls) and social action (feeding of bodies and minds), and all that that has done is to nullify the impact of God's redemptive plan on a dying world. In the English—speaking Caribbean region, the nation that is recorded to have the most churches per square mile simultaneously records skyrocketing crime rates, with murders becoming a daily way of life and "garrison communities" which have become impregnable. How do we stop this swirling tidal wave of madness from drowning us completely? How do we persuade governments to assume their God-given role as keepers of peace and dispensers of justice, and how do we develop citizens to accept the responsibility of freedom?

Myles Munroe as already noted calls us to true freedom—a freedom that demands hard work. As a people who have been colonized, oppressed and enslaved, we must begin to increasingly respond to the burden and responsibility of freedom:

> True freedom comes from moving into the responsibility of crossing over Jordan in personal accountability to God and His Word. Jesus has proclaimed it and opened our prison doors, but we must take the responsibility to walk outside and be free. The decision is made in the mind". [He boldly asserts,] "the major dramatic difference we see between freedom and slavery is the fact that freedom is much harder to engage because of personal choice and responsibility . . . freedom demands more work than slavery.[112]

Today the call goes out to Caribbean peoples to catch God's vision of a new agenda, to lay hold of the real meaning of biblical spirituality—a spirituality which has God as its source and centre based on the truth of Who God is and what He asks of us His children and creation.

The type of spirituality propounded by Jesus Christ is described by Conn not as an *"evangelistic escape from history but a participation in the new reality of history"[113]* brought about by the redemptive work of Christ and the application of God's Holy Spirit in the daily living-out of our God-given mandate—a new spirituality of change. He goes on to note:

> . . . to be interested in things spiritual is to be interested in all of life, now touched by the healing hand of the Holy spirit. It is to be interested in the things that interest the Lord, to have our hearts broken by the things that break the heart of God . . . God's . . . call to discipling nations, the work of Christ's Spirit in creating the new life of the kingdom come . . . is a call to grace, God's response to man's sin that man may fulfil God's call to culture building.[114]

Conn further comments: "This new day of the Sprit has everything to do with social involvement . . . . At Calvary, Jesus united evangelism with His work of restoring society. He broke the chains that shackled the world's cultures to their own sins; justice and mercy meet and kiss each other at the blood-sprinkled throne of grace we call Golgotha."[115]

It is therefore, from wearing the spectacles of the above worldview that I call the Caribbean region to action. The model that follows is not an end in itself. For me, it is the beginning of a long run homeward. Some have already started; others of us are just getting set to take our place at the mark, ready to join the running conversation and catch up with friends. The model constitutes some ideals that we all long and yearn for, based as they are on God's Kingdom principles of integrity and synergy, character and competence, courage and consideration, simplicity and stewardship, culture and community, reconciliation and participation. The vision required to turn the tide around is a vision of character. It is a vision of the heart for a vision of character is a vision of the heart. Jim Wallis puts it very well when he declared:

It is a renewal of the heart to which we are now summoned. The crisis of the times calls for our conversion. Our structures, values, habits and assumptions are in need of basic transformation. Neither politics nor piety as we know it will effect such a change. Rather a new spirituality . . . a spirituality rooted in old tradition but radically applied to our present circumstances.[116]

The models I present seek to further our search for a new vision of change.

DEVELOPING A WHOLISTIC MODEL

This work is an ambitious attempt to develop a strategy for change and to encourage the emergence of a practice necessary to effectively communicate this vision for change. What I am seeking to do through this effort is to integrate several theories/concepts of change into an interrelated whole. Too often the propositions offered on change deal with one, or perhaps two aspects of individual and/or organizational behavior. The human is however body, soul and spirit operating in spiritual, physical, economic, cultural, social and political spheres. I am deeply challenged to seek to bring together a number of theories that I find particularly compelling, in the design of a model for change. What I hope will happen is a continued honing and refining of these ideas, through discussion and dialogue, critiquing and improving on models offered in ways that would spread their understanding and encourage a decentralized movement for change among people. I claim no ownership of the concepts that I will be exploring over the following pages. I do, however, feel a strong sense of kinship and partnership with the authors of these ideas, whose writing have made a considerable impact on my personal life and have gone a long way in shaping my vision of the world. I believe that they are worth sharing in the manner in which I propose to present them. My sincere hope is that it will in some small way contribute to the growing search for meaningful alternative models for change. Our world is changing rapidly. It may not be in the way that we desire nor envisage. With some considerable effort and no little energy however, we can seek to steer more strongly and stably, through mounting waves and thundering winds, the ships of unrelenting change. Although I can promise no safe ports, I dare predict some greatly strengthened passengers.

The proposed model examines four types of change: **psycho-spiritual, religio-cultural, socio-political** and **socio-economic**, focusing on the individual, the society, the community and the market place. A number of concepts have been identified to reflect the types of changes proposed. They are Principle-centered, Character-based Leadership (Covey 1989, 1990), Soul Force (Ellis 1983), Community Governance (Peck 1987, 1993), and Stewardship (Block 1993). Some core values of change have been identified as underpinning both theories and types, namely integrity, love, unity, empowerment and justice. I appeal to readers of this short discourse to be patient with me, even in areas of distinct disagreement. I will make every attempt to be open and inclusive because I am convinced that it is only in and through emptiness and tolerance that one can find the real path to authentic change.

PSYCHO-SPIRITUAL CHANGE:
PRINCIPLE-CENTERED LEADERSHIP

Many successful attempts have been made to combine psychological and spiritual growth. There is increasing recognition that both areas of study have much in common; namely, the growth in inner reality and maturity of the human person. While psychological maturity has to do with growth in self and other-consciousness—some may say the development of the soul (the mind, the emotions, and will); spiritual development is concerned with the maturing into meaningfulness and purposefulness of the human potential. For some religious traditions, spiritual growth involves growth in God-consciousness, development of the divine spirit in the human. I have chosen Stephen Covey's theory of principle-centered, character-based leadership within a psycho-spiritual context because it deals specifically with growth of inner character-change in the inner person, in meaning, in purpose, in perception and in behavior. It begins with change in self. Here Covey states it very well,

> The deep, fundamental problems we face cannot be solved in the superficial level on which they were created. We need a new level of thinking based on principles . . . to solve these deep concerns. We need a principle-centered, character-based, inside-out approach. Inside out means to start first with self, with your paradigms, your character, your motives . . . if you want to be trusted, be trustworthy. If you want the secondary greatness of public recognition, focus first on primary greatness of character.[117]

Any meaningful model for change must begin at the level of the self—in the individual person, in the individual country, the particular village, the specific community. We have wasted much time and resources attempting to change others, to change structures, institutions and systems while as individuals in our family units and in our organizations we have remained unchanged. We have externalized our problems, sought for scapegoats, while we refuse to accept the work and challenge of change. We have avoided the important task of self-awareness, while we clamour for others to be gender and environmentally aware. We really are about the business of changing others not ourselves. We fight to overthrow the oppressor while we have retained in us the very values and attitudes that breed oppression. We live our lives without integrity—yet shout loud accusations at the corrupt and dishonest, that are in positions of power. Good people refuse to take leadership; yet we are surprised when the less dishonorable emerge and take charge. We live in terrible contradiction and our worlds system is convulsed in the same painful confusion and dissonance. Our scientists, economists, feminists, environmentalists, and political analysts are all working feverishly on new and viable alternatives to save the planet earth. The leaders of the world sit down in summit after summit. The declarations which emerge are visionary, the plans of action very reasonable, though all too often not achievable. So, our social and physical environment continue to deteriorate, human relationships disintegrate, national and regional crises escalate and personal values degenerate.

Our society displays a frightening loss of character. This did not happen by chance or overnight. Charles Colson noted that

> Societies are tragically vulnerable when the men and women who compose them lack character. A nation or culture cannot endure for long, unless it is undergirded by common values . . .; it cannot stand unless it is populated by people who will act on motives superior to their own immediate interest. We have failed to develop as a people of principle-centered values. We have nurtured within our families, communities, organizations, competitive individualism, flagrant inequalities, compromising relativism and greedy materialism. We have produced societies of people without chests. Communities without souls and culture without character.[118]

Can we stop this downward spiral into decadence, decay and death? Can we put an end to the injustices, abuse and violence that surround us? Can we really eliminate deprivation, dispossession and poverty as we are aiming to do? (World Social Summit 1995/Millennium Development Goals), Can we resist and fight the terrifying dehumanization of personal lives, especially among our youth, the relentless entropy of our family and community life and the awful destruction of our societal processes and physical environment? The answer must come from each and every one of us—not only with the politician, pastor and principal, as important as these leaders are. We the adults and older youth of the country and region must begin to take personal responsibility for our lives based on principle-centered values.

All around the world, there are important and innovative processes for change taking place. One such process is being worked on by Stephen Covey—professor, public speaker, and now, well known author. Two of his more popular books, *The Seven Habits of Highly Effective People* (1989), and *Principle-Centered Leadership* (1991), have been used widely in training in personal and organizational leadership. In his model of development, Covey stresses a character ethic as the way toward change, seemingly, lost values such as humility, fidelity, temperance, industry, simplicity, modesty and the golden rule underpin his propositions. Permit me to share briefly on his *Seven Habits of Highly Effective People*.

Habit One proposes a personal vision of proactivity and responsibility. It means taking responsibility for our attitudes and actions. Proactive people develop the ability to choose their response, making them more a product of their values and decisions than their moods and conditions. The more we exercise our freedom to choose our response, the more proactive we become. This habit teaches us to concentrate more on our immediate circle of influence rather than the larger circle of concern.[119]

Habit Two focuses on personal leadership. The habit of personal leadership means to begin each day with a clear understanding of your desired direction and destination. Management is concerned with efficiency. Leadership is concerned with effectiveness. Effective people realize that things are created mentally before they are created physically. They write a mission or a purpose statement and use it as a frame or reference for making decisions. They clarify values and set priorities before selecting goals and going about their work. Ineffective people allow old habits, other people, and environmental conditions to dictate their mental creation.[120]

Habit Three posits personal management—putting first things first and prioritizing one's goals. Personal management involves organizing and managing time and events according to the personal priorities of Habit 2. Urgent things usually act on us. And we usually react to them. But we must be proactive rather than reactive to do the important but not urgent things. Only by saying no to the unimportant can we say yes to the important.[121]

Habit Four points to interpersonal leadership, thinking win-win and seeking consensus. Win-win is the habit of interpersonal leadership. In families and businesses, effectiveness is largely achieved through the cooperative efforts of two or more people. Win-win is the attitude of seeking mutual benefit. Win-win thinking begins with a commitment to explore all options until a mutually satisfactory solution is reached, or to make no deal at all. It begins with an abundance mentally—enough for all to share. The win-win performance agreement clarifies expectations by making the following five elements very explicit—desired results, guidelines, resources, accountability and consequences.[122]

Habit Five promotes empathic communication which seeks first to understand and then to be understood. The habit of emphatic communication is one of the master skills in life, the key to building win-win relationships and the essence of professionalism. We see the world as we are, not as it is. Our perception comes out of our experiences. Most credibility problem begins with differences in perception. To resolve these differences and to restore credibility, we must exercise empathy, seeking first to understand the point of view of the other person. Emphatic listening is deeply therapeutic because it gives people physiological air; once people are understood, they lower their defences.[123]

Habit Six which talks about the principle of creative cooperation, encourages synergy and teamwork. Synergy is the habit of creative cooperation or teamwork. For those who have a win-win abundance mentality and exercise empathy, differences in any relationship can produce synergy, where the whole is greater than the sum of its parts. Synergy results from valuing differences, by bringing different perspectives together in the spirit of mutual respect. People then feel free to seek the best possible alternative, often the third alternative, one that is substantially different from and better than either of the original proposals. Synergy is the human resource approach to problem-solving.[124]

Habit Seven concludes with the principle of balanced self-renewal, "sharpen the saw". The habit of self-renewal undergirds all the other habits of successful people. The habit of sharpening the saw regularly means having a balanced, systematic program for self-renewal in the four areas of our lives: physical, mental, emotional/social, and spiritual. Without this discipline the body becomes weak the mind mechanical, the emotions raw, the spirit insensitive and the person selfish. It is the law of the harvest; we reap as we sow.[125]

We will enjoy a successful harvest if we cultivate these seven habits of effectiveness and live in accordance with the underlying principles. Principle-centered values as articulated by Covey are not ends in themselves. They are means to an end. Indeed they are simply tools to be used as we seek to transform ourselves, our communities and societies into people and places of character and integrity. This transformation is, of course, of a largely transcendental nature—it is deeply spiritual in essence. Like others of the Judeo-Christian tradition or Biblical worldview, I believe that **God** who created **man** and **woman** in His own image and likeness, is the ONE capable of truly transforming our natural self-will into loving other-centeredness, and our normal bent to destructive behavior to that of creative endeavor.

At this particular juncture in our Caribbean history, one finds enormous disillusionment among the population (old and young). The pervasive mistrust of our major social institutions, including the church, but more particularly the institution of politics, is alarming. Governance is in crisis; leadership is in disarray. Families are disintegrating. Very recently (2010), I found one of my old journal entries dated April 1987 where I noted nine (9) marriages that were in trouble and for which I was praying for healing and reconciliation (all parties were still together), to date, all but two of those marriages have been legally dissolved. I was totally dismayed at the road we had travelled over the years. We are in serious trouble! Of particular concern is the obvious absence of a vision of change. We dare not move further into the twenty-first century without beginning to deal with these urgent issues and concerns.

In this model of principle-centered leadership/character, **integrity** is the core value. It is where we must begin—an acceptance of ourselves—who we are, where we came from, and what we have become. As we seek to embrace the value of integrity which does not simply mean honesty, but rather an integrated character—a oneness of self and life, we come to the humble realization that we cannot handle life on our own; that one truly finds oneself, only when one is willing to lose one's self. Scripture puts it thus: " . . . unless a kernel of wheat falls to the ground and dies, it remains only a single seed" (John 12:24 NIV). Principle-based character is formed on values that are transcendent, values that reflect the very laws of a Personal and Infinite God Who loved so much He gave . . . . Jesus, the God-man gave His life that we may live. And whether we articulate our faith with clarity or not, whether we share differing traditions and belief systems, as we move closer and closer to the heart of God and to these transcendent values, we gain increasing grace to become individuals, families, communities and cultures of character.

RELIGO-CULTURAL CHANGE: SOUL FORCE

Weakened characters produce a sick culture. Our culture is sick and needs to be healed. This is not an exaggerated, emotional notion of the writer. Indeed, people all around, from a variety of walks of life are talking, writing and singing about the sickness of our society. This sickness is reflected in the way we think, the choices we make, the goals we pursue and the way we relate. We are often more interested in cash rather than character, in charisma than in competence. We pursue self-interest over service. Too many of our youth are bent on self-destruction, attention-getting behavior. Our calypsonians are so disillusioned that their lyrics border on destruction. Our women are so disempowered that they have lost all sense of dignity. Our young men are so emasculated that they seek to find themselves in anti-social, illegitimate activities and experiences. All around us crime rises, moral values decline and families fragment. This is not hysteria!

We may choose to believe that it's hysteria because many of the old assurances still surround us. We commemorate our independence; we memorialize our heroes. We elect our governments; we debate our budgets. We display with pomp and ceremony our parliamentary processes and our church rituals. We graduate our students and christen our babies. We celebrate with musical gusto and grand pageantry our festivals and carnivals. Yet the crisis looms as a darkening cloud which we dare not ignore for "The crisis is in the character of the culture, where the values that restrain inner vices and develop inner virtues are eroding."[126] Furthermore, it is the conviction of many that the crisis is not simply economic or political but is largely moral and spiritual and thus demands moral and spiritual solutions. Indeed though now deceased, William Demas, renowned Caribbean economist wisely noted that it is not grand economic planning and growth that will fulfil our hopes for a better life, but change within ourselves and in our social values.[127] It is important to quote at length Demas' words:

> The critical area in which change is required is in that of values.
> Only a change of values would hold out hope for a solution of the
> unemployment problem for transformation of agriculture and
> rural society. Only a change of value would enable the people

to accept a revised definition of development . . . only a change
of value could contain the revolution of rising expectations for
material improvement. Only a change of values could give the
people the motivation to build from below.[128]

The change which is therefore proposed at this level is <u>religio-cultural</u>. It
combines religion (a belief system with demands for faith) with culture
(the collective consciousness of a people). It is ethical; it is moral, as
well as practical and material. In this discourse, the religio-cultural
change articulated comprises of four specific characteristics: One, it is
three-dimensional; two, it is God-centered; three, it seeks to provide a
balanced view of history, our present situation and of destiny; and four, it
attempts to respond to a quest for freedom and dignity. Each dimension
will be briefly elaborated.

Carl Ellis tells an interesting story of some people who lived in a country
called Flatland. In this country people lived only in two-dimensions—north,
south, east, and west. They never understood about up and down. One
day someone came to talk to them about a three-dimensional world. She
told them that she came from above. Of course, they neither understood
nor believed her because for them whatever was inconceivable in their
two-dimensional world must be impossible. Despite the efforts of the
visitor, she could not engage the Flatlanders in a meaningful discussion
and because they insisted that Flatland was the ultimate reality, they
ended up with a distorted view of reality.[129] The worldview of the secular
humanists is likened to the view of the Flatlanders.

The Biblical or Judeo-Christian worldview posits that there are two parts to
reality—the natural world—that which we see and the supernatural—that
which we do not see. The late Francis Schaeffer pointed out that "reality
has two halves, like two halves of an orange. You do not have the whole
orange unless you have both parts. One part is normally seen, and the
other is normally unseen."[130]

Much of our theories, ideas, plans, policies and practices are committed
to the concept of the uniformity of natural causes in a closed system.
The natural reality is for us the only reality. We live in a two-dimensional
system—the natural world. For the naturalists, the supernatural world,

because it cannot be seen, not only is it unscientific, but it is downright foolish. Therein, we seriously err. Carl Ellis in discussing black militant secularism advocates that it was a limited perspective which left God out of the picture of the world. He felt that such a limited viewpoint was propagated in the interest of religious neutrality. It was felt that people could talk about history, change, science, civil rights, and human rights, while ignoring the reality of God. Moral decisions were therefore strictly individual in nature.[131] Again, they erred. Ellis noted sadly that "the secular militants ended up merely switching from a God-centered religion to a man-centered one—secularism and humanism."[132] He reasoned that while there may have been justification for rejecting "white Christianity-ism" and replacing such with definitions of their own, the militants simply replaced God and became the ultimate judge of right and wrong. What resulted was degeneration in attitudes and behavior and disintegration in relationships and organization.[133]

A religio-cultural change that works, must not only be three-dimensional and supernatural, but must be decidedly <u>GOD-CENTERED</u>. In being God-centered, we recognize that we are created, finite beings. We acknowledge that there is true truth, that there is an Infinite God of the universe. A God who created heaven and earth (above and below), and who created human in His own image and likeness. The Judeo-Christian articulation of a Personal, Infinite God, Who is all Spirit and Who is both Creator and Maker of the human and of history, informs the posited notion of God-centered change. This proposition begins with the God of the universe Who made man and woman in His/Her own image and likeness, and made a natural world of order and predictability.

This God of the universe set out in written propositional truth (*the word of God, the Bible or Holy Scripture*), the way of life—abundant life, which often meant sacrificial, other-centered living. The Mighty God of the universe also set in motion an organism called the church, which is in essence a living community, a living body of spirit-controlled people, each with a personal commitment to live life on His terms of God-centered values that adhere to a transcendent standard of right and wrong. Indeed, God the Creator ordained <u>three major institutions</u> for the ordering and maintaining of societal values: <u>The family,</u> beginning with a **man** and a **woman**, for the procreation and nurturing of new life, <u>the state</u> for the preservation and protection of human life, and the church for the proclamation and practice of His word of life. When these institutions move away from their God-centered calling, the decay and eventual death of a culture results! The only way back to health and wholeness of a culture, of a society, must lay in the restoring of these institutions to their rightful roles of consciousness-raising and character-building, life-protecting and justice-promoting, and God—and other-serving. The religio-cultural change which is God-centered must therefore take as its starting point God's point of view and must have a vision that encompasses the secular and the spiritual, the natural and the supernatural, the evil and the good, the awfulness of human sin and the wonder of God's grace.

The religio-cultural change as proposed seeks to bring balance to our way of life by providing a new way of looking at history, our present life and our destiny. Caribbean people must look back from where we have come, what the significant events of our past are that have shaped who we are today as a people. What are the psycho-social as well as spiritual meanings of our journey? What in our past has been forgotten, exaggerated or distorted and why? Most importantly, what are the lenses through which we look back—is it secular humanism, radical feminism, revolutionary Marxism, or balanced God-centeredness? It makes a huge difference which perspective we take. We have tragically erred by leaving God out—the results: significant omissions, faulty prescriptions and painful consequences.

History and destiny are for us what the third—dimension was like to the Flatlanders. As limited finite, human beings, we cannot by ourselves without God's help understand the full flow of our history. Similarly, we lose our sense of direction or destiny without God as our unfailing guide. God alone, as Infinite Maker and Creator of history, can unerringly guide us through its flow to our final destiny. Caribbean people, especially youth, are perplexed and confused about the way forward and doubtful and disillusioned as to where we are headed. Over the past several decades, we have in a variety of ways sought to integrate our efforts, combine our resources and unite our people—our attempts so far have had very limited success. As the world becomes smaller and smaller though, the need to clarify our past and to chart our destiny becomes even more urgent. We

Joan M. Purcell

can only do so however, as we seek to understand and define who we are today.

How can we as Caribbean people begin to define ourselves? How can we know whether our collective consciousness—our standards and values, traditions and mores—is healthy and life-affirming? What yardstick do we use to test the soundness and sustainability of our present reality? The religio-cultural model for change proposes a worldview based on God's inerrant Word as the litmus test of our present reality. It posits a worldview which stresses moral absolutes, unchanging principles, and deep religious commitments as the basis for shaping and defining the past, present and future. Only by seeing ourselves as God sees us, will we avoid false, self-destructive values . . . and a distorted view of reality. A Godless reality or ungodliness results in a distorted reality; a distorted reality leads to "*a kind of cultural death.*"[134]

The last characteristic of religio-cultural change deals with the central human quest for freedom and dignity. It is noted that when God is left out of our worldview and framework for action, ungodliness results in character and culture. One of the important battlefronts on which struggle is waged today is against oppression—a fight for freedom. People everywhere are fighting either to gain or regain freedom, or to preserve and/or protect the freedom that is theirs. The black people of South Africa paid dearly for their freedom. The history of the Caribbean tells its own story of our bitter quest for freedom and dignity. Today, women are waging an often cruel battle against oppressive systems and structures. Ethnic and indigenous groups are struggling for a place in the sun. North and south, east and west, the story of struggle and resistance is the same.

The fight for human dignity is indeed a spiritual fight. And this is so because the only real basis for human dignity comes from the biblical teaching that the human is made in the image and likeness of a transcendent God. Our dignity is therefore derived from God's dignity and any loss of that dignity is a spiritual loss. If the Creator God gives meaning to human dignity, then Carl Ellis is again correct when he states, "It is God's grace alone which provides the basis for resisting oppression. It is His grace which provides the power to resist oppression. It is God's grace which provides the will to resist oppression. If we leave God out, we leave out the very possibility of liberation."[135]

A religio-cultural approach to change attacks the very root of cultural oppression. It speaks of true liberation not license; it speaks of freedom from the oppression of others, not freedom from the control of Almighty God. It speaks of LOVE as the basis of that control, and SOUL FORCE as the medium of expression for the moving into God's love and for transmitting a people's resistance to evil and ungodliness. The concept of "soul force" comes of course from Carl Ellis, who has been quoted quite frequently. He introduces the concept of soul force along with the ideas of soul dynamic and soul culture in discussing the historical black American resistance to oppression and their journey to freedom. Ellis describes soul force as *an indigenous theological outlook and practice*[136] which was based mostly on the oral tradition of black people in their struggle to survive.

According to him black people during slavery, transformed the Bible from its written form into an oral form using "soul culture." They produced a "theological dynamic" that captured nuggets of biblical truth in forceful phrases and images of life experiences, creating "a cultural dynamic of deeply moving expressions of black consciousness reflecting the image of God in us."[137]

The Caribbean experience could no doubt, be described in as graphic a way. Black people of the Caribbean, up to today, seek to translate their struggle to survive in songs, dance, drama, art, poetry and calypso, reggae and steel-band. These all resonate up from the soul seeking to declare to the world our consciousness of ourselves—as a people, as a free people, as a people with dignity, as a culture with character. You have only to listen to the internationally known Grenadian Calypsonian, Black Wizzard.[138] Wizzard is described as "a lyricist par excellence," as he sings *Struggle(1980), The IMF (1989)* and *Massa(1994)*—lyrics that have today not lost any of their relevance and potency as social commentaries. Listen also to the powerful Psalmist, Caribbean Woman of God, Reverend Angela Williams as she calls on "Elohim," "He's reigning in the hearts of His people, He's reigning in the islands of the sea, He's reigning, the Lord of the nations . . . ."[139]

We have not been faithful however. We have allowed our culture to be penetrated, undermined, downgraded, degraded and despised. We have failed to be good stewards of our soul dynamic. Often we have accommodated evil rather than fought it. We have allowed ourselves to be divided and ruled. We have frequently been selfish and hostile to each other. We have by and large forgotten our cultural heritage rather than proudly declared it. We are suffering from cultural anorexia and historical amnesia. The God of the universe is however beckoning to us. Calling us out of conformity! Calling us not to be escapists or defeatists! God Almighty, the Sovereign Creator, loves diversity yet represents the highest order of perfect unity. God calls us through the rightness of our soul dynamic, through the recklessness of our soul force, through the reality of our soul culture to accept His gracious gift of <u>love</u>. He gives us hope to keep our vision intact.

He gives us a song in our heart and puts strength in our hands to do the costly job of deconstruction and redemption as the late Bob Marley sings in his redemption song: *my hands were made strong by the hands of the Almighty; we forward in this generation triumphantly.*[140]

SOCIO-POLITICAL CHANGE—COMMUNITY GOVERNANCE

Socio-political change is about change in the power relationship among people. It talks about how power is defined, used and shared. It is inextricably linked with both psycho-spiritual and religio-cultural change. It seeks to empower people, to build community, to transform institutions, to heal society.

The core value of socio-political change is UNITY—out of which comes the very important concept of **community**. Come let us make unity! The burden of this discussion is to forge a strong relationship between **politics** and **community.** Indeed the Lausanne Covenant (1974) defined politics as *t*he art of living in community. The politics of community, or community governance is the model proposed for change. The best proponent of this theme (as far as I know) is M. Scott Peck—popular author, lecturer, psychiatrist and founder of an organization called Foundation for Community Encouragement. Dr. Peck in his books, *The Different Drum* (1987), and *A World Waiting to be Born* (1993), describes with great depth of feeling the ideal of community. According to him "in and through community lies the salvation of the world . . . nothing is more important."[141]

Present day politics is however characterized by anti-community. Tribalism and divisiveness are the hallmarks of partisan politics. Character assassinations are hailed as the ultimate weapon. Mystification and unreality are promoted as creeds. The more unreal the promises, the greater the political fervor they elicit. It all adds up ultimately to a crisis in governance. Governments renege on promises. Party groupings are marked by splinterization. In the December 1984 National Elections of Grenada, over eighty percent of the electorate voted to take the country back to democracy after the demise of the Grenada Revolution(1979-1983). The New National Party (NNP), led by the now deceased Honourable H. A Blaize, formed the Government. By December 1989, five years later, that same party was splintered into three in readiness for new elections: The New Party—TNP (led by H.A. Blaize), New National Party—NNP (led by Keith Mitchell) and National Democratic Congress—NDC (led by George Brizan). As a result of the pervasive nature of partisan politics, communities become increasingly fragmented. Unrealistic expectations result in disillusioned, disempowered and discouraged people, and desperate, defeated politicians.

Governance is indeed in crisis! And do we recognize the crisis? The majority of us do, although we may view it from differing perspectives. Peter Block in examining responses to change, identified three groups of people—the cynic, the victim, and the bystander.[142] The same dynamic is seen to be in operation in our responses to the crisis in governance. The cynic is convinced that it is hopeless, no matter what is tried—*"they are all the same, nothing good can come out of politics."* The victim constantly clamors for a change in *who* governs, not for a change in the system of governance—*"this is the worst government, let us give this man a try!"* The bystander is not prepared to take responsibility or to make any commitment but may or may not go along with the crowd—*"I'm not interested in politics."*

Is there any way out of this self-defeating cycle? Undoubtedly there is. The way out is, however, neither easy nor comfortable, neither alluring nor popular. Indeed, it is risky, fraught with difficulties, open to failure, but definitely challenging and life affirming. It is by and large untried. But oh, it beckons us to come, come away, move away from our comfort zone to new levels of thinking and being, willing and acting. According to this proposition, this movement requires: a real understanding of the meaning of community and the process of community-making with a clear recognition of the nature of reconciliation and its implications for leadership.

I spent sometime in the previous discussion on *Recreating Structures* in elaborating on the Meaning of Community, especially as articulated by M. Scott Peck. Some of which bear repeating! Community as a concept is used rather loosely and has different meanings for different people. Scott Peck sees community-making as an inherently mysterious, miraculous, and unfathomable process. Therefore to capture its essence in a single definition is inadequate. He sees the seeds of community as residing in humanity, and, like gems, community becomes possible through a process of cutting and polishing.[143]

Real community though difficult to describe, does carry certain intrinsic characteristics. Peck identifies three: inclusivity, commitment, and consensus.[144] If community is to be real, it must be willing to extend itself and to struggle with the widespread phenomenon of exclusivity. It must be aware and appreciative of the full range of human differences and human experiences and be prepared to celebrate them. This of course requires commitment to work together regardless of individual differences. It involves a willingness to coexist and a preparedness to stick together when things are tough. The same transcendence that takes place at the individual level must take place in community as people's attitude toward each other change and where alienation is transformed into appreciation and reconciliation.

Scott Peck identified certain stages in community-making: Pseudo-community, Chaos, Emptiness, and Community.[145] **Pseudo-community** is the first response in seeking to form a community. Members are extremely pleasant to each other. All efforts are made to avoid disagreements. People fake community at this stage. Everyone pretends that they share the same values and beliefs and individual differences are neither acknowledged nor admitted. The goal is to avoid conflict at all cost and to create instant community. Pseudo-community is conflict-avoiding; true community is conflict-resolving. Most groups and organizations remain in this stage for a considerable length of time.[146]

The state of **Chaos** is entered when people begin to admit individual differences. People move to greater honesty. It is, however, a time of fighting and struggling—noisy, uncreative and non-productive. This is so, for although differences are recognized and admitted, there is no real acceptance of differences. Unlike, Pseudo-community where attempts are made to hide or ignore differences, in chaos, the goal is to obliterate differences—attempts are made to convert each other. According to Scott Peck, chaos is not just a state, *it is an essential part of the process,* and must needs be experienced before one can move on.[147] Indeed, the view is held that fighting is far better than pretending you are not divided.

There are two ways out of chaos: one is organization—*"let's form a sub-committee to deal with this issue"*. Organization, however, is **not** community. The preferable route is that of **Emptiness.** This is an extremely critical stage. It is the bridge between chaos and community. This is also a very difficult stage. It is that place where one empties oneself of barriers to communication—expectations, preconceptions, prejudices, ideology, solution and most of all, the need to control. It involves the painful death of self—self-protection, self-interest, and self-importance. It is the transformation of a collection of self-centered individuals into a group of other-centered people.[148]

When its death has been completed, open and emptied, the group enters COMMUNITY. It is a time of peace, vulnerability and inclusivity. It is also a period of creativity and problem-solving. The group is at its most productive. The process is *"Community*-building first, problem-solving second."[149]

The politics of community governance demands a radical change, nay, transformation in the way politics is viewed and the manner in which it is done. Today, politics is seen as a game; it is often presented as a drama of images—a politics of image building and of what looks good, what sounds good—a politics of expediency. A skilful 'wheeler-dealer "and master 'machinator'" are seen as mandatory to the process. To move from this unreality, both the leadership and follow-ship must change. Leaders of government must become committed to the principles and spirit of community and community-making, based on realism and integrity. People's expectations of Government must also involve a significant shift. The super-man, must be replaced by a realistic understanding of governance and the responsible role of the body politic.

Referring to my own experience as a leader in government and member of cabinet, I recall, as mentioned in my Memoirs (2008), that leadership of a small, open, developing state,

> required extraordinary leadership, involving **courage, competence, compassion,** moral **conviction** and true **community** . . . my personal evaluation of our period of service (1990-1995) is that while we performed creditably in the first four c's above, we failed dismally in the final and most important "c" above, we failed dismally in the final and most important "c"—community. A recurring failure in the politics of Grenada! I dare say in the world.[150]

I will now attempt to define, perhaps more accurately, describe what I intend to convey when I propose *Community Governance* as an alternative approach to governance in our region. As stated previously, the notion of bringing *community* and *governance* together has, for me, been best articulated in M. Scott Peck's vision of a "community presidency."[151]

My intent is to extend this vision in a way that reflects the Caribbean's "Westminster" model of governance which comprises the executive branch of Prime Minister and Cabinet and the Parliamentary arm made up of elected and appointed members of government and opposition.

Community governance is an *approach* to governing which includes the two-fold elements of *selection* of a group of persons to govern and the *operation* of that group. It is not a system or institution. While all of our Constitutions today are crying out for reform, this approach is not so much about form and structure as of spirit and process. It is indeed a *process* and it *does* require a change in one's worldview of how one governs. This change involves both the manner in which a government is selected and the way that group operates when elected. Firstly, this approach mandates that individuals who present themselves to the electorate must be chosen "not so much for their particular expertise as for their capacity to operate in community . . . ; in other words candidates would begin by developing an effective community . . . ; in short, from the very beginning of the electoral process the people would be voting not simply for an individual but for a community".[152]

Indeed, I can well recall in my first national election experience of March 1990. We, the candidates of our party, the National Democratic Congress, presented ourselves to the electorate as *a team*—the Best Team to take Grenada forward. The tragedy of this action was that we had never entered into community. We assumed that teamwork and consensus decision-making would emerge as we competitively carried out our duties to our constituencies and argued over scarce resources. We never learnt to "fight gracefully." We failed to do beforehand the hard work of moving from pseudo-community, to chaos through emptiness into real community. And I have seen history, very recent history, repeat itself again and again. We have largely ignored the lessons of the past.

Secondly, once teams are elected and appointed (government and opposition), these teams must continue to function as a community for "all major decisions [are to] be made in community and consensually."[153] This community of persons will have a high tolerance for conflict. It will be truly inclusive and not subject to 'cliqueism'. It will call for emotional and spiritual maturity and the acceptance diversity. It will creatively include the official Opposition, who will themselves be a community, in the task of governing.

This radical shift in the way we do politics will call for healthier governments and civil society. This of course is a process and will take time. But we must start somewhere. It would require a group of persons truly committed to health and wholeness in governance, sincerely convicted about spiritual authority and Godly strength, and boldly courageous to attempt such a revolutionary shift in spirit. Yet it is precisely such a shift in spirit that is needed in our politics and governments today. It requires a transcendent worldview!

In the proposed model of community governance, the process of education and training, comes before a team presents itself to the electorate. This means, too, that the electorate, through widespread community and public education, must come to the place where it will accept no less from its leaders. This vision of community governance must be thoroughly explored and widely shared with the electorate. People will be encouraged to vote not for individuals but for a community of leaders. Persons, who have worked together, have come into community and are willing to operate in community. Such a shift from the traditional way of doing government will no doubt be revolutionary, but nothing less than such a shift can save us from total disaster. Grenada, the Caribbean, the World, needs a vision that can turn the world upside down; it took only a handful of people to do it some two thousand years ago. It can be done again!

I do not wish to leave readers with the impression that community governance is a panacea to all our socio-political challenges and that it will usher in a type of utopia. That type of promise only comes with the fulfilment of God's Kingdom *"on earth as it is in heaven."* (Matthew 6:10b KJV). It is, however, offered as a reflection of and ongoing movement toward God's perfect plan for this earth. The reality is that the process of moving into community is dynamic and ongoing. It is also spiritual. It is not a once for all event. I wish to reiterate that it is a dynamic process, full of risks and vulnerability and involves hard work and discipline—values which are desperately yearned for by an electorate of its leaders. Scott Peck reminds us that "community maintenance requires that multiple major decisions be made and remade over extensive periods of time. The community will frequently fall back into chaos or even pseudocommunity in the process. Over and again it will need to do the agonizing work of re-emptying itself. [154] My humble submission is that in spite of the risks, there is simply too much at risk— the very survival of our Caribbean civilization as 'nations with souls' — for us to dismiss, without serious reflection, this vision of community governance.

I wish to briefly touch on the critical issue of *reconciliation in* community-building and the leadership required for such a process. The theme of reconciliation could require several chapters. This work does not afford me such latitude, but I could not conclude this section without this short exploration. Closely linked to the concept of community is the principle and practice of reconciliation. Reconciliation, like community (unity), is a biblical concept. Human beings are divided among themselves and separated from God. The practice of reconciliation is to bring people together in unity and in community. Today our Caribbean communities are crying out to experience this process of reconciliation, whether it is to deal with the political tribalism which exists in Jamaica and Grenada; whether it is the racial divisions of Trinidad and Tobago and Guyana; whether it is the class divisions and gender inequality which can still be found in all of our nation states. The evils of social exclusion, social inequality and divisive politics are very real and only a genuine process of reconciliation can turn the tide around.

Garnett Roper comments on the local and regional situation in this way:

> There is little doubt that this is a region and a society in severe crisis. The rate of violent crimes, especially murder has created a climate of instability and fear. The effect of the global realities in the global financial systems as well as the inheritance of high national debt and fiscal imprudence has put the livelihoods of the majority of citizens at risk. In addition social exclusion and social inequality have been deepening and are exacerbated among Caribbean people. Jamaica for example has sixty per cent of its high school cohort leaving schools without passing a single subject. The society has become accustomed to more than twenty per cent of its youth male population becoming gang members, there is high unemployment among young women. This has led to a higher incident of public disorder and social dysfunctionality.[155]

Can there be any doubt that the Caribbean as a region requires a quality of leadership and governance that will bring hope and restoration to nations which God has so richly blessed both with human and natural resources. Reconciliation is not optional. Our divided communities cry out for healing. It must be noted, however, that reconciliation is neither integration nor accommodation. It is definitely not politically correct language. It is neither an emotional high that we get when we join hands and sing "Bind us together Lord." It is the stretched-out hands between a Holy God and sinful humanity. It is inclusion. It is a value: who we are, versus what we do. It is the way forward in moving beyond guilt and blame and establishing us as a new family of brothers and sisters. It is the politics of unity. **It is community!**

H.P. Spees sees leadership as the key to achieving reconciliation and identifies three types of leadership as crucial in achieving Godly reconciliation: *open leadership*—leadership from the dominant culture or group, that is open to change; *new leadership*—leadership from among the disenfranchised culture, minority groups, e.g., women, indigenous peoples; *bridge-builders*—leadership that is cross-culturally adept and able to sensitively bridge the barriers which separate people.[156] The search for such leadership to facilitate and provide integrity to the process must be the goal of those of us interested in true reconciliation.

I think it is fitting for me to conclude this section with some challenging words from Scott Peck—words which articulate so well what I would like to leave with my readers concerning the birthing and nurturing of an alternative vision. He notes,

> The gulf between what is and what needs to be is so great as to make these proposals seem like a dream. The so-called realists may call it "naïve". The prophets of the old brain will scream "impossible". "It is a mere feckless vision", they will say . . . but they, the prophets of the old brain, are the prophets of death . . . for . . . where there is no vision, the people perish.[157]

SOCIO-ECONOMIC CHANGE: DEVELOPMENT AS STEWARDSHIP

Significant socio-economic change must come if we are to survive. This level of change, as the other levels already elaborated, is posited to be as crucial to the region's development and sustainability—each level needing the other for maximum impact—all interlinked and interdependent. The socio-economic change here proposed is articulated as **Development as Stewardship** meaning management of our God-given resources in ways that all would benefit. Christian apologist, the late Francis Schaeffer pointed out that human beings are given the responsibility by God to act as stewards over His creation, to protect, preserve, develop and use for the good of humankind and the Glory of God.[158] Darrow L. Miller sees Stewardship as "creating and managing bounty." [159]Bounty, for him, is God-given abundance: "Stewardship in the physical realm involves progressing in God's story toward the City of God—tending His creation so that it becomes increasingly fruitful."[160] Human beings are co-creators with God. "Man, made in God's image, is given the awesome task of bringing forth all the potential of creation. Man is the source of earth's bounty as well as its poverty.*"161*

Miller goes on to show the link between **development and stewardship.** Indeed he states, "development, understood as stewardship, maintains a dynamic tension, between conserving and progressing*"162* This is a stark contrast to secularism and humanism which progress without conserving or animism which conserves without progressing. The under-development and un-development of this world, therefore, lie squarely in our hands; the more we as humans follow God's laws and principles, the richer the resources we produce. The converse also follows: the more we take ownership and control of God's earth, abuse and misuse earth's resources, the more shattering and tragic the destruction. Take for example the gift of technology. Yes it is a *gift* from God to His created order, to create wealth for His creation. Nonetheless, "the problem with technology is that it has been separated from morals. Cut from their transcendent moorings, we are adrift in a 'brave new world', full of pollution, dehumanization, and death . . . . Man loses his place in the universe and becomes a slave to technology.*"163*

Peter Block, in his book entitled *Stewardship—Choosing Service Over Self-interest,* explains that his book is written with the intent of reforming organizations so that democracy thrives, the spirit is answered and the ability to serve customers is guaranteed; it is about "living out democratic values using the workplace as the focal point.*"164* His use of the concept of **stewardship** as the key to organizational change is very appealing. He sees Stewardship as the key to organizational growth and development and a direct challenge to the prevailing patriarchal system of governance of our institutions.[165] Block elaborates:

> Stewardship is the set of principles and practices which have the potential to make dramatic changes in our governance system. It is concerned with creating a way of governing ourselves that creates a strong sense of ownership and responsibility for outcomes at the bottom of the organization. It means giving control to customers and creating self-reliance on the part of all who are touched by the institution. **The answer to economic problems is not more money; it is to focus on quality, service and participation first.** This is what will put us closer to the market place . . . **an economic crisis for any organization** (and here I would include governments) **means failure in its marketplace. In some fundamental way it is unable to serve its customers** [Emphasis mine][166]

Indeed, within the countries of the Caribbean, it is noted that the ones with the most money or natural resources are the ones with the greatest problems. The answer must lie outside of money. Our governments today are experiencing acute problems in managing our small economies, a situation which is translated into problems of unemployment and underemployment, low productivity, low wages, high cost of living, inefficient bureaucratic structures, outdated management systems, low worker morale and prolonged industrial disputes. People in and out of government are clamoring for reform. Both public and private sectors are feverishly seeking new economic agendas. Our several attempts at restructuring appear to be more palliative than preventative, more reactive than proactive. **We need genuine alternatives.**

Stewardship, as one such alternative, in its commitment to **service,** moves us from the role of parenting (our workers, constituents, electorate, economic sectors and customers) to that of **partnership,** from dependency to **employment,** from management to **governance.** Governance, here, means how purpose is defined, how power is held, and how wealth is distributed. The view is put forward that our economics will remain in crisis unless there is genuine reshaping of our institutions' purpose, power and wealth along lines that eschew the existing form of "intimate colonialism" and benevolent paternalism and move to embrace more participatory, creative modes of governance.[167]

Stewardship is a governance strategy. And while stewardship covers concerns of the spirit, it must also pass the test of the marketplace. Block sees it as both practical and economic. He notes the existing fight for survival in the marketplace:

> Higher quality of goods and services, lower costs and rapid innovation determine our survival. The governance system . . . cannot deliver quality, costs too much, and is ill-suited to meet the need for rapid change. Patriarchal institutions cannot serve their customers. Therefore they essentially fail in the marketplace, and economics is the measuring rod for their failure. Schools only teach a portion of their students, government perpetuates helplessness and futility in its constituents . . . . business and industry all seem to hang in the balance. The marketplace for each institution is its reality. To embrace stewardship, choosing service over self interest, is to join the testing ground for integrating personal and economic values and making the spirit concrete and practical . . . the revolution is . . . about the belief that spiritual values and the desire for economic success can be simultaneously fulfilled.[168]

While Block's central focus is on corporate stewardship, Rifkin espouses a far wider view of the stewardship doctrine. Rifkin sees the newly emerging stewardship doctrine — one that is diametrically opposed to the old theory of "dominion", meaning to manipulate and exploit — as a fundamental critique of the modern world view which includes centralization of power, technological excesses to meet consumer demands, fragmentation of labor, devastation of the environment in the name of progress and other such goals.[169] Instead he states,

> Stewardship requires that humankind respect and conserve the natural outworking of God's order. The natural order works on principles of diversity, interdependence, and decentralization. Maintenance replaces notions of progress, stewardship replaces ownership, and nurturing replaces engineering . . . the

new stewardship doctrine represents a fundamental shift in humanity's frame of reference. It establishes a new set of governing principles for how human beings should behave and act in the world.[170]

The concept of Stewardship says people do matter. It says people are infinitely more than matter. We are central to God's design of the world and anything—even if it is seen as progress—which pushes people aside, which replaces people with machines has to be anti-human. An economic model where people matter and which incorporates the outworking of the Stewardship covenant means "adopting living patterns that make us partners of nature rather than its exploiters."[171]

The type of living proposed in this alternative economic model is found in a life style where all people matter—not just a few, not just a race nor a class. Although our resource base may be limited, although we are often faced with growing demands and expectations, we can and must do a better job at ensuring greater levels of equity and economic <u>justice</u> for our people. The principle of stewardship as a means to development directly confronts our deeply entrenched economic values of unregenerate materialism and unrestrained technological progress. And despite the contradictions and convolutions which we are experiencing today—within the first decade of the twenty-first century, every effort will be made to retain the status quo and to leave intact the institutions and systems that have captivated the hearts and minds of our people. Doubtless, substantial skepticism and considerable resistance will be offered at any attempt to change these entrenched values. But with determination and courage, with humility and openness, with love, faith, and hope, we **must** forge ahead if we are to provide a future to the next generation. Undoubtedly, it will involve a long process of change which will include not only economic structures and choices, but also socio-political goals and aspirations, religio-cultural vision and mission and psycho-spiritual principles and values.

Today we take the first step into the future. What will it be?

PART 1V

FAITH, POLITICS
AND
LEADERSHIP

THE CORNERSTONES OF THE VISION OF CHANGE

The Just shall live by faith
(Romans 1:17 KJV)

I wish to begin this short discourse with this bold assertion: "if one is to have a mature politics, one must have a mature faith. If one is to be a mature leader, then one must be mature in faith." In the following pages, I will seek to provide some thoughts on the validity of the above claim. I hope to join in the ongoing conversation or provoke some fresh conversation that will refine and define the themes of Faith, Politics and Leadership as crucial elements for the earth's healthy renewal and survival. The triple themes of Faith, Politics and Leadership have evoked my considerable interest, enquiry and reflection, especially as they pertain to the arena of community— building and sustaining. Over a quarter of a century, I've studied all three topics and found them to be interlinked, interrelated and interdependent. Therefore, I have chosen as the cornerstones of this Vision of Change—Politics, Leadership and Faith—a three-legged stool equipped to hold the weight of transforming communities and contributing to human well-being. In this proposal, *politics* builds community, *leadership* serves community, and *faith* offers transcendence and meaning to community.

You may ask why my emphasis on community building, community serving and community transforming. What is it about community that can bear the weight of the world's healing or more accurately be used in service to bring healing and wholeness?

My answer goes back to the source, nature and meaning of community. M. Scott Peck, one of North America's most passionate proponents of community-building, boldly asserts, "In and through community lies the salvation of the world . . . . Community is a spirit . . . the spirit of community is inevitably the spirit of peace and love".[172] Darrow L. Miller in describing the nature of community strongly characterizes it as "One, Yet Many!"[173] He describes community as "the radical middle" which has "a metaphysical starting point: **the Trinity.** "[174] According to him, "societies that find this balance value both freedom (which emphasizes the individual) and justice (which emphasizes the community)." [175]

The Biblical worldview presents the "three-in-one" God, the "One and Many" God, the **Triune God**, Father, Son and Holy Spirit, God in perfect community—God as a community of Persons exemplifying both unity and diversity! The truth of the One-in-Many Godhead, the Biblical Trinity holds radical implications for our society and for our economic and political life. Miller quotes British Economist Brian Griffiths who states that, "*the* idea of community is crucial to the life of society. "[176] Griffith notes the deficiency of any society that sees the individual as an automaton and fails to capture the significance of relationships. Equally deficient is the failure to embrace the notion of unity in diversity: "In the Trinity the one God does not take precedence over the many persons, neither do the many have priority over the One. " [177]

In political terms, when the One is given preference, totalitarianism results; so too when the Many is placed first, anarchy is the logical consequence—with both being translated into their economic equivalents. In the "radical middle," the Trinitarian way, where the one and the many are properly balanced, where there is unity in diversity, where the rights of the community are held in tension with the rights of the individual, justice and freedom are the divine imperatives. This is God's intent for His world! The "radical middle" requires faith, a radical faith, a "theodependent" faith which acknowledges God as Supreme and His rule over our lives as Sovereign and total. A faith which sees what is not yet visible, knowing that the visible proceeds from the invisible is required.[178]

This Faith gives energy and motivation to vision and will inspire risk-taking action. It is a faith which is willing to die to self so that others may live. It is also a faith which produces humble servant leaders, welcomes the mystery of community and the strength and wisdom of unity. A Leadership of faith operating in political community is the cornerstones of a vision of change. A faith that dares to dream!

THE IMPERATIVE OF FAITH

For centuries, faith appeared to be the sole province of religion and provided meaning and direction for peoples and cultures. The advent of modernism with its attendant secularism, pluralism and relativity "have all cracked and fissured the mosaics of meaning by which whole cultures have been formed and sustained."[7] Into this hopeless vacuum, people are seeking ways and means to secure a shelter of shared values that will provide protection against an onslaught of meaninglessness. Today, I wish to return to religious faith, and in particular Judeo-Christian, biblical faith as a way of life in and out of our hopelessness.

In recent times, an interesting alliance appears to be forged between religious faith and politics (US Presidential Elections 2004/2008). Stephen Mansfield gives an interesting account of Barak Obama's incredible impact at the Democratic National Convention in July 2004:

> For those who listened to the speech with an ear for the overtones of faith, there was a single sentence that signaled a defining theme in Barak Obama's life . . . "We worship an awesome God in the Blue States" . . . Though the words are but nine among more than two thousand, Obama intended them as a trumpet call of faith. No longer, he was saying, would the political fault lines in America fall between a religious Right and a secular Left. Instead a Religious Left was finding its voice: We, too, have faith, they proclaimed . . . we also love God. We, too have spiritual passion, and we believe that our vision for America arises from a vital faith as well. No longer will we be painted as the nonbelievers. No longer will we yield the spiritual high ground . . . Barack Obama was raising the banner of what he hopes will be the faith-based politics of a new generation and he will carry that banner to whatever heights of power his God and the American people allow.[179]

In November 2008, it carried him into the White House, a historical and trail-blazing event! I can well remember that evening in 2004, sitting with my brother Sam in my tiny family room in Tempe, St. George's, Grenada, when hearing, for the first time, Barack Obama, in that fateful speech. My brother prophesied, "that man will go far; Joan, watch out for him." Of course, I was deeply impressed with that young, tall, skinny, black man with the funny name, but never dreamed that that man's faith which fuelled his vision would have such an impact on the people of America, and the world for that matter. According to Mansfield, "he is unapologetically Christian and unapologetically liberal, and he believes that faith ought to inform his politics and that of the nation as a whole."[180] And so do I believe. As Paul Tillich sees it, faith is the courage to be and to become. It is the state of being ultimately concerned. It is the act of the total personality and happens in the center of the personal life and includes all its elements.[181]

Fowler gives faith a developmental thrust. He provides a graphic articulation of faith:

> . . . faith is a human universal . . . wherever we find human beings, our species is marked by several uniform features and dimensions of struggle and awareness . . . the universal awareness of death . . . the burden of having to make life-defining choices under conditions of uncertainty and risk . . . we have imaginations, intuitions, and moments of awakenings that disturb our awareness of dimensions . . . that we can only name, on our own, as "mystery". And yet our feet mire in the clay of everyday toil in the struggle for survival and meaning . . . we are language-related, symbol-borne and story-sustained creatures. We do not live long or well without meaning. That is to say, we are creatures who live by faith.[182]

In our ongoing journey of self, faith is a primary motivating power; it shapes the responses we make in life's force-field and constitutes the core element in character development.

Permit me to spend some time on Fowler's characterization of faith as the operations of knowing and valuing and its stages of development. My very first encounter with Fowler's work over two decades ago, left me excited and intrigued, as I sought to wrestle with my own growing faith. It made sense. Fowler identified through primary research, seven sequential stages of faith, each representing a different pattern of faith knowing. The first four stages, Primal Faith, Intuitive-Projective Faith, Mythic-Literal Faith, and Synthetic-Conventional Faith, usually take place by adolescence. The last three stages are seen to be an exclusive phenomenon of adult development—Individuative-Reflective Faith, Conjunctive Faith and Universalizing Faith. Fowler emphasizes the structural characteristics and not so much the content of faith.[183]

M. Scott Peck, though admittedly less precise in his approach, grounds his position on "noncomputing" experiences.[184] Basing his work on Fowler's six stages of faith, he refined them into four stages of spiritual growth as he names them. At the beginning or bottom is the "chaotic/antisocial" stage—a stage in which spirituality is absent—people are utterly unprincipled. It is antisocial because one can pretend to be loving; relationships are self-serving and manipulative. It is chaotic being led by unharnessed wills, lawlessness. While people in this stage may be frequently in trouble, some may be quite self-disciplined in the service of ambition and may rise to positions of considerable power and prestige.[185] History attests to many such community and world leaders. Persons may, in this stage, destroy themselves, or be converted to stage two.

Stage two, labelled "formal/institutional," provides a safe place for persons who are dependent on an institution for their governance. It is often the Church. Having being converted from stage one, persons may remain in stage two for most or all of their lives. Stage two people often fear change, are legalistic and wedded to stability.[186]

Stage Three, the "sceptic/individual" describes one who is often "not religious in the ordinary sense of the word," is socially oriented and truth seeking. One may find doubters, agnostics and atheists at this stage. But as seekers of truth, they move into another stage and some of the myths of stage two may begin to take on new meaning.[187]

In the fourth or final stage, according to Peck, "mystical/communal"—the most mature of the stages—persons become comfortable with mystery, observe "the spirit of the law". They do not fear paradox and welcome community.[188]

Peck elaborated on some points worth noting regarding spiritual growth or faith—development as I would call it. It is possible to "backslide" into a lower stage if one is not yet properly grounded in the advanced stage, but it is not possible to skip over a stage. And no matter how far one develops, a person still retains vestiges of the earlier stages and may revert to them under stress or crisis. One never arrives! Stage Four is simply "the beginning"! The beginning of a life of maturing faith!

While Tillich's view of faith is concerned with being and becoming, and while Fowler and Peck have described the process of faith as knowing and making of meaning, traditional religious writers on Christian faith have emphasized the *belief* component—the content of faith. To this I will now turn my attention.

Faith in the Biblical/Judeo-Christian tradition begins with a belief in a personal, infinite God Who has revealed Himself propositionally and historically. It constitutes ultimate dependence on a God Who is there and Who is not silent. Christian faith is not a leap in the dark. It is not faith in faith. It is faith in a God Who has content. It is believing in the power, providence and promises of an Ultimate and Sovereign God.[189]

Charles Colson clarifies, *"This faith requires no surrender of the intellect. It is not blind, unthinking, and irrational. Nor is it simply a psychological crutch."*[190]

Kao describes Christian faith as having both cognitive and affective components. The cognitive aspect of faith is belief in certain doctrines and forms of propositional content about the Ultimate. Affectively, it is identical with trust and commitment which signifies "the internal integration and unification of our psychic energies into a single channel . . . faith is the key that releases invisible (and divine) power within a person who is divided and at odds with oneself . . . faith liberates a person from the agony of inner conflicts and gives new birth of one's personality." [191]

Bouwsma sees faith as beginning with an acceptance of one's creature-hood. It begins with the realism that humankind's only source and resource is the will and grace of a loving God: "By faith man is dramatically relieved of his false maturity—his claims to self-defined 'manhood', and enabled to begin again to grow."[192]

Permit me to return to a brief exploration of James Fowler's discoveries and descriptions on the structural features of faith, with focus on the fifth and sixth stages, individuative-reflective and conjunctive faith, as these have very direct bearing on my intended discussion on Leadership.

Individuative-Reflective faith, Fowler states, comes into being "by a variety of experiences that make it necessary for persons to objectify, examine and make critical choices about defining elements of their identity and faith."[193] In this stage the individual must begin to take seriously the burden of responsibility for his/her own commitments, life-style, beliefs and attitudes. Two shifts must take place. One is an evolution of self-authorization and emergence of an "executive ego," and the second a critical examination of beliefs and values and the making of choices regarding these.[194]

The next stage, the fifth, Conjunctive faith involves "the integration of elements in ourselves, in society and in our experience of ultimate reality that have the character of being apparent contradictions or polarities."[195]

Fowler identified five hallmarks of the transition to Conjunctive faith: (a) an awareness of the need to face and hold together several unmistakable tensions in one's life; (b) an awareness that truth is more multiform and complex than was previously seen, being conscious of the apparent contradictions of perspectives on truth while one is able to accept and attempt to understand these paradoxes; (c) a genuine openness to the truths of traditions and communities other than one's own, without the need to respond to differences and contradictions by accepting relativism; (d) the willingness to commit oneself to transformation toward a more inclusive truth which transcends the inadequacy of any contradicted vision; and (e) the ability to avoid reifying symbols of truth but rather with humility to grasp that any offer of ultimate truth that one's traditions provide needs continual correction and challenge.[196]

In order to give life and meaning to the above discussion, I will provide descriptions of the journey into faith of Barak Obama as provided by

Stephen Mansfield in his book, *The Faith of Barak Obama* (2008), and excerpts of my own life as described in"Naked and Unashamed: A Journey into Faith and Maturity"(1986) an unpublished paper written by myself. Mansfield notes that Barak Obama's faith was fashioned from the hard-won truths of his spiritual journey:

> He was raised by grandparents who were religious sceptics and by a mother who took an anthropologist's approach to faith: religion is an important force in human history—understand it whether you make it on your own or not. Nurtured as a child in the warm religious tolerance of the Hawaiian Islands and the multiculturalism of Indonesia in the late 1960s and early 1970s, he grew into a young man for whom race was more of a crisis than religion. As the son of a white American mother and a black African father who left the family when Barack was only two years old, he felt too white to be at home among his black friends, and too black to fit easily into the white world of his grandparents and mother. He was a man without a country.

> Ever the emotional expatriate, he was haunted by displacement through his college years and through his troubling experience as a community organizer in Chicago. It was not until he rooted himself in the soil of Trinity United Church of Christ on Chicago's South Side that he began to find healing for his loneliness and answers for his incomplete worldview. He experienced for the first time both connection to God and affirmation as a son of Africa. He would also be exposed to a passionate Afrocentric theology and a Christian mandate for social action that permanently shaped his politics. Through Trinity, he found the mystical country for which his soul had longed.

> Yet he also found that through this country flowed a bitter stream. As he quickly came to understand, Trinity Church's broad Christianity was permeated by a defining, if understandable, spirit of anger: toward white America, toward a history of black suffering, toward a U.S. government that consistently lived beneath the promise of her founding vision.

If Obama himself refused to drink from this bitter stream, he was mentored by one who did.[197]

Kicking and screaming, mentally and emotionally, Barack Obama came to Church!

> A man of doubt and conflict. The sermon that day was on a topic that would live in his soul and in his politics. It was called "The Audacity of Hope". In the skilled rhetorical hands of Jeremiah Wright, the lessons mounted into a grand symphony of uniquely African-American preaching. Searing biblical content was overlaid against social commentary and brought to bear on the sufferings and promised victories of each individual life in the congregation . . . Despite the broad range of references, or perhaps because of them, a laser of hope penetrated Barack's soul. At sermon's end, he found himself in tears. It was the beginning. The process that followed took months.

> It was a decision to enter a faith by joining a people of faith, to come home to a community and so come home to God. Indeed, as Obama has explained, "It came about as a choice and not an epiphany; the questions I had did not magically disappear. But kneeling beneath that cross on the Sought Side of Chicago, I felt God's spirit beckoning me. I submitted myself to His will and dedicated myself to discovering His truth. [198]

Barak Obama is a political being, led and guided by his faith—a faith which no doubt he finds *today* more complex and multiform than he may have thought; a faith which must be constantly questioned and challenged; a faith where mystery abounds and humility is found—a 'becoming son' before an All Loving Father!.

I would now like to share some excerpts of my own journey into faith as recorded in 1986:

> Viewed from the spectacles of Fowler's stage of Conjunctive Faith, I recall with great clarity the struggles and tension,

conflicts and confrontation which developed within me and between others and me involved in my journey of faith.

I found myself confronting the powerful pillars of traditions in the church and those persons who had elected themselves as upholders of these traditions. The struggle was more intense because these external conflicts ran parallel to the internal conflicts of coming to terms with those deep paradoxes that make up real life.

I will mention a few of these struggles for meaning and integration . . . I struggled to find the meaning of Christianity in revolutionary, political and social change. I was struck by the apathy, hypocrisy, escapism and other-worldliness of those of us who professed to believe in a God of Justice, peace and love. Whose side was God on—was it the poor and the oppressed; was He for the upholder of the status quo (many of whom were the most dedicated "Christians" and church-goers); was He for the radical revolutionary, often arrogant but who appeared to have the courage to identify what was wrong and to take the risk to make changes?

I challenged myself, my fellow believers and the church hierarchy. By the church I was viewed as liberal; by the radicals, I was seen as un-progressive. The loneliness and vulnerability of this position forced me to some definite resolution.

I agreed wholeheartedly with Moustakas that "new awareness opens amidst anger, fear and despair . . . when devastating experiences of confusion and rejection can be turned into opportunities of self-realization".[199]

Both on a personal and community level, I was forced to re-examine the role of women in the church. I could not with honesty and integrity accept the symbol of the meek, quiet, unassuming woman which was portrayed in our churches . . . I looked around and saw hundreds of women seemingly repressed and 'trapped' in a community in which we are called into freedom and abundant living . . . I recognized that as Christians we were abrogating our right to be the "salt of the earth" and "light of the world", when we allowed evils and injustices to go unchallenged while we indulged in pietistic posturing.

I also became concerned with issues of Peace and Development. My country had experienced a war! It was both preceded and accompanied by violence, pain, death, bitterness, division, disillusionment. The illusion that I lived in a peaceful, idyllic part of the world was rudely shattered. Global issues of international sovereignty, justice and peace were now part of my reality. The people of Grenada were confused, divided and without leadership. I had to find answers. I had to face the paradoxes and contradictions and come to terms with them and with myself. I had to find out more about the world around me. It was not simply survival of one small, for some reason significant island in the Caribbean, but of the world—the entire human race, where the drama of hate, violence and war was played out day by day.

In all of these struggles, I began to look more seriously at the Christian tradition, and the ways it had been presented to me, to my people. I felt impelled to examine more closely the history of black people, our own history, and the methods and motives in the presentation of Christianity. I became interested in reading Black and Third World Development writers. Issues on Liberation Theology, Christian Feminism, Black Theology, Peace and Non-Violence, became my particular focus—throughout the journey a number of new 'meaning perspectives' developed.

A strange paradox was taking place within me. The more disillusioned I grew with 'Churchianity' and 'Christianitism', the more my faith in God grew, and my love for Jesus Christ deepened. I began tentatively to reach out to a God Who is vastly bigger, more mysterious, more loving, just and compassionate, Who was calling me into partnership with Him, to work, on myself, with others, and in institutions and structures to bring about His Kingdom. His Word, the Bible, became a book of love letters to a loveless world.

I began to learn slowly that our world needs both "lovers" and "prophets".

I am indebted to Keith Miller for this distinction. According to him, "lovers" are those who would be concerned with addressing the personal sense of isolation and the need for love and esteem which motivate all people in whatever situation and structure they find themselves. "Prophets" are those who have the guts and insight to confront forces and power structures in political activities as well as the personal and social agony of their country and their world.[200]

I learned in my struggle that God was calling me to be both prophetic and loving. I think that this lesson was extremely important because one can so easily see them as mutually exclusive. In being prophetic, it is easy to become unloving and intolerant. In being loving, it is just as easy to be compromising and placatory. They are both necessary in a life of faith, though perhaps to differing degrees.[201]

Today, I continue in my pilgrimage of a maturing faith. It continues to be beset by real feelings of fear and uncertainty at the awesome responsibility, risks and costs involved in attempting **not to be** sparing in one's caring, selective in one's choosing and safe in one's calling. Fowler warns of the reality of fears and insecurities as finite persons in a dangerous world of power, and the importance of maturing faith which brings with it *"a powerful fearlessness in the face of the imperatives of absolute love and justice,"*[202] such as is found in his final stage of Universalizing faith, reached by few, if any. Such is the faith, however, displayed by Jesus Christ, the Son of God, Who "became flesh" to show us the heart of God and Who today I utterly trust to strengthen my "mustard-seed" sized faith.

In conclusion, Faith is an imperative in our quest for meaning. Faith is indispensable in our search for hope. Faith is the vehicle that leads to love.

Mature faith opens the door to healing. Our world today desperately needs, in addition to prophets and lovers, 'faith—full' *healers.* Women and Men of Faith! Leaders of Nations! Political Statesmen and Stateswomen! People of God! Persons who trust a Sovereign Omnipotent God to direct and guide, teach and instruct, lead and inspire, strengthen and encourage. From where do such persons come? Mansfield provides an answer:

> They tend to come after bruising, bloody seasons, and yet they seem immune to the rage and vengeance of lesser men. They know how to grasp forgiveness and generosity of heart, having usually mined these traits from the dark valleys of their own lives . . . they rise to grace a public stage and then heal their land and their people with the truths hard-won in less-visible day.[203]

Great is the need for such **political leaders** of **Faith**!

THE CHALLENGE OF POLITICS

Charles Colson in acknowledging the limits of politics to bring about genuine political reform, quotes former British Prime Minister, Margaret Thatcher as she addressed the General Assembly of the Church of Scotland:

> The truths of the Judaic-Christian tradition are infinitely precious, not only, as I believe, because they are true, but also because they provide the moral impulse which alone can lead to that peace . . . for which we all long . . . . There is little hope for democracy if the hearts of men and women in democratic societies cannot be touched by a call to something greater than themselves. Political structures, state institutions, collective ideals are not enough. We parliamentarians can legislate for the rule of law. You the church can teach the **life of faith** (emphasis mine).[204]

This takes me to the question, how can the *rule of law* and the *life of faith*, "the body politic" and the "body spiritual" find common ground?

Serious thinkers and writers have spent much time wrestling with this issue. Scores of answers have been provided, discussed and debated. Some have been debunked, others have been embraced. I strongly concur with Charles Colson in his examination of this dilemma, when he concludes, "By his nature man is irresistibly religious—and he is political. Unless the two can coexist, mankind will continue in turmoil."[205] He goes on to note regarding the ongoing struggle and tension between church and state, *the cross and the crown*, which he sees as inevitable, "The critical dynamic in the church-state tension is separation of institutional authority. Religion and politics can't be separated—they inevitably overlap—but the institutions of church and state must preserve their separate and distinct roles."[206]

So while one acknowledges the tension, the crucial importance for the institution of the church to provide a moral mandate and imperative to the institution of government cannot be dismissed. Through vocational leadership, men and women in politics living a life of faith can provide this indispensable moral authority. Some of the most outstanding and impactful men and women of politics have been people of faith.

William Wilberforce (1759-1833) knew that he could not with integrity, passion and endurance work for the abolition of slavery without having a strong faith, based on a calling from a Compassionate God Who hates oppression. "He knew that a private faith that did not act in the face of oppression was no faith at all."[207]

Abraham Lincoln (1809-1865), one of America's most influential and impactful leaders, a statesman and a healer, in the midst of national crisis, was clear in his vision of faith, "And having thus chosen our course, without guile, and with pure purpose, let us renew our trust in God, and go forward without fear and with manly hearts."[208] Indeed he strongly exhorted, "Let's have faith that right makes might, and in that faith let us to the end dare to do our duty as we understand it"[209]

Abraham Kuyper (1837-1920), Dutch politician, journalist, statesman and theologian, and founder of the Anti-Revolutionary Party, as Prime Minister of the Netherlands (1901-1905), articulated the heart of his calling: "When principles that run against your deepest convictions begin to win the day, then battle is your calling, and peace has become sin, you must, at the price of dearest peace, lay your convictions bare before friend and enemy, with all the fire of your faith"[210]

Martin Luther King Jr. (1929—1968). His commitment to justice could not be understood apart from his faith. According to Carl Ellis, Dr. King saw biblical ethics applying to every area of life. His ethics apologetic was universal.

> [He had] a love ethic like Jesus, a cultural brilliance like Paul's, a poetic speech like Jeremiah's, an agenda for justice like Amos', a direct-action drama like Ezekiel's, and a mode of Leadership like Moses'. God had spoken to Brother Martin:
>
> "God has spoken to me, and I'm not going to run from the responsibility!
>
> May mean going through the floods and through the waters, but I'm going if it means that!
>
> May mean going through the storms and the winds, But I'm going if it means that! May mean going to jail, but I'm going if it means that! It may even mean physical death, but if it means that I will die standing up for the freedom of my people!
>
> God has spoken to me.[211]

"Faith is taking the first step even when you don't see the whole staircase,"[212] so said a man of faith who lived by faith and died in faith.

Malcolm X (1925-1965), a Muslim minister and radical activist, spent the brief years of his life struggling against racism in the United States. It is noted that his vision for social justice, especially in the final years of his life was rooted in religious faith. He is described by Deyoung as a *"faith-inspired activist"*[213] who lived his faith and who also died in faith.

Corazon Aquino (1933—2009), a woman who for a brief moment in history turned the tide around, from power-hungry politics to people's power leadership, provides yet another insight of politics lived through a *life of faith.* She was pressed into service in her country, the Philippines, after the brutal murder of her husband Benigno Aquino in August,1983, on his return to his native land to struggle against the then Marcos dictatorship.

> Cory Aquino, in her calm, firm, common-sense manner—just the opposite of a glib, polished, professional politician—seemed to embody democracy. She was a housewife pressed into politics by the need of her nation . . . in front of the vast assemblage spread like a colored mosaic at her feet . . . she did not send them to storm Malacalang Palace—though they would have gone.

> She asked them for a day of prayer . . . (and) for a series of nonviolent protests . . . This simple housewife with **faith of iron** narrowly survived several coup attempts while she grappled to get control of a government that had been almost wholly corrupt." Her secret, "Cory Aquino was at perfect peace. "I didn't seek this . . . I only want to serve my people. I simply have to put my trust in the Lord." I had the impression she would face death as resolutely as had her husband.[214]

Nelson Mandela (1918—), a man who spent twenty-seven of his best years incarcerated and fighting for his life and his country against one of the most inhumane systems, Apartheid, states, "I knew that people expected me to harbor anger toward whites. But I had none. In prison, my anger toward whites decreased, but my hatred for the system grew. I wanted South Africa to see that I loved even my enemies while I hated the system that turned us against each other."[215]

A man whose faith had been tested, who confessed that at times during his long imprisonment his faith in humanity was sorely tried, came to the unshakeable conclusion:

> . . . my hunger for the freedom of my people became a hunger for the freedom of all people, white and black. I knew as well as I know anything that the oppressor must be liberated just as

surely as the oppressed. A man who takes away another man's freedom is a prisoner of hatred . . . . the oppressed and the oppressor alike are robbed of humanity.[216]

He acknowledges that it is a long journey, "the first step on a longer and even more difficult road. For to be free is not merely to cast off one's chains, but to live in a way that respects and enhances the freedom of others . . . with freedom comes responsibilities, and I dare not linger, for my long walk is not yet ended. "[217]

Aung San Suu Kyi (1945—), known throughout her native land, Burma, as "The Lady," an affectionate name given to her by her people because she encompasses all the hopes and dreams of her Burmese people. She is described as "a faith-based leader who has embraced the ethics of revolution that says systemic change in society requires an internally driven change in values. " She said: "Without a revolution of the spirit, the forces which produced the iniquities of the old order would continue to be operative, posing a constant threat to the process of reform and regeneration."[218]

Tillman Thomas (1947-), a Gideon of the twenty-first century, humble, simple, inarticulate, except when exploding against injustice—the Prime Minister of Grenada Carriacou and Petit Martinique from July 2008. A man of faith; a leader who has lived out the courage of his conviction, being imprisoned for several years (1979—1984) by the then Revolutionary Government of his country, for his stand for press freedom!

Tillman Thomas in his commitment to serve his country with transparency, inclusivity, accountability and honour chose to work with persons who were responsible for his unjust imprisonment. His forgiveness of them resulted in his leadership of a political party and government which included several of his opponents of the past.

He is strong in faith, simple in lifestyle, and a liberator of his people from years of unethical governance.

Such are our leaders of valour! To whom will they hand the baton of political leadership of this global village? Where are our vocational leaders today? Men and women who are called—called to lead with integrity and honesty. Alas, they are few and far between; the exception rather than the rule. Our leaders have bought wholesale the notion that politics is raw power. We fight to "get into power". But where did this notion come from?

We turn now to examine some view points on politics. Robert C. Tucker in his insightful book entitled, *Politics as Leadership,* explores the differing viewpoints on politics. He examines the classic view of politics, which dates back to Plato, which sees politics as "the pursuit and exercise of power in the interest of those who pursue and exercise it. "[219] Tucker elaborates on Plato's later dissenting view of politics as statesmanship: "The true Statesman, possesses knowledge of what is good for man, is a physician of souls . . . as shepherd of the human flock. Statesmanship . . . [is] the art of tending the flock." [220] Tucker laments, however, that the power approach to politics has had a tenacious hold over time upon thoughtful minds, and concludes that we are paying a steep political price for our preoccupation with power as the be all and end all of politics: "Viewing politics as power has blinded us . . . to the pivotal role of leadership."[221]

Tucker points out that although political leadership has largely been leadership for power; there are political leaders for whom power is mainly an opportunity to exercise leadership for ends other than power—several of whom, I have cited above. He draws on Max Weber's exposition of *Politics as a Vocation* where politics is defined, in essence, as leadership or attempted leadership of whatever is the prevailing form of political community. Politics as leadership is not the exercise of power for power's sake. According to Tucker, politics as a leadership process is more comprehensive than the "leader-for-power" approach. The former conception of politics as leadership involves the recognition that whatever interest there is in power, something that will always figure in political life: "politics is basically a realm of the mind. "[222] He believes that people as individuals and as leaders particularly "make a significant difference in historical outcomes by virtue of the ways in which they act or fail to act at critical junctures in the development of events."[223] History is therefore open ended. How political leadership is done "matters in history." Tucker asserts the following:

"The process of political leadership is activated when circumstances take on meaning for a political community, and a political problem is recognized. Leadership (then) has the three-fold task of diagnosing the situation authoritatively, devising a course of action designed to resolve or alleviate the problem and mobilizing the political community's support for the leaders' definition of the situation and their prescribed policy response."[224]

While Tucker deals very persuasively with his concept of political leadership as acting, doing, being competent (ideas with which I have no argument), I would like to expand on an additional dimension of political leadership: it is a *calling*, a *vocation*. Here, I would like to lean rather heavily on the work of M. Scott Peck in *A World Waiting to be Born*. Scott Peck sees vocation as far more complex than what one does for a living; he explores the religious meaning of "what one is called to do which may or may not coincide with one's occupation."[225] Peck explains what he understands about vocation:

Vocation implies a relationship. For if someone is called, something must be doing the calling. This something is God. As a Christian, I believe that God calls us humans beings—whether skeptics or believers, whether Christian or not—to certain, often very specific activities. Furthermore, since God relates—covenants—with us as individuals, this matter of calling is utterly individualized. [226]

Scott Peck believes, however, that every human being is called to be civil, to "psychospiritual growth;" he defines civility as "consciously motivated organizational behaviour that is ethical in submission to a Higher Power".[227] And goes on to note that the more conscious one is of one's calling, the more one will be able to cooperate with God in His plan; and the more one can match one's true vocation with one's occupation, the more civil one will be.[228]

In expanding on the concept of civility, Peck identifies three "interlocking cornerstones:" (1) the civil person being ethically conscious of other people, individually and collectively, as precious beings, (2) the belief that humans are so precious because they are created by a divine and Higher Power, reflecting in themselves some of the divinity of their Creator, and (3) the need for the civil individual to be in a relationship of willing submission to that Higher Power.[229] He elaborates:

> Just as consciousness is ever expanding, leading us to the awareness of an ever larger system, so civility is an ever-expanding process. It is but a small step from seeing people as precious by virtue of their Creator to seeing all creation as precious. The practice of civility inevitably leads us into larger systems, ecological consciousness, and a loving concern for the integrity of the whole.[230]

It is to this vocation—this calling, I hear the urgent, desperate cry of *a world waiting to be born*. A call goes out bidding the response of true political leadership, pleading the appearance of "priestly politicians," urging the emergence of courageous civil leadership and entreating the manifestation of men and women called to political leadership on this our beloved planet. It is a call for men and women who are prepared to put soul into politics. It is a call for men and women with the *"second naivety"* of childlikeness—an apt description by Leonard Hulley and others of Archbishop Desmond Tutu. This *"second naivety"* is described as:

> an intuitive grasp of reality which arises out of experience, a knowledge of good and evil, indeed a knowledge of human nature, (the) ability to keep hope alive in the future when the political analysts have already determined that there is no future . . . a gift . . . a grace . . . (which) is not a denial of reality nor an escape of reality—it is a different way of relating to reality. Only the childlike have the **faith** which moves mountains.[231]

The question is from whence comes this **faith**? And this takes me back to the issue of religious faith and its relationship to politics? Doug Bandow in his exploration of a Christian political perspective reminds us of the following:

religion and politics have been intertwined throughout recorded history. Whether the belief be paganism, Judaism, Christianity, Islam, or atheism, the faithful have often looked to the state for support and sustenance. Even in today's increasingly secular world, many of the worst cases of regional conflict and sectarian strife . . . . Israel and its Arab neighbours, Northern Ireland . . . involve nationalistic struggles for religious supremacy.[232]

While there is major disagreement and debate, especially in Christianity, as to the role and relationship of politics and religion,, increasing effort is today being made by Christian writers, scholars and social activists to prayerfully think through and act out the proper relationship between Christianity and politics in the modern world.

I found the article by Kevin Rudd (former Australian Prime Minister) entitled, "Faith in Politics" as particularly informative and insightful. Rudd in his essay honours Dietrich Bonhoeffer (1906—1945), German theologian, peace activist, *"man of faith . . . man of reason . . . man of action"*,[233] whose writings sixty years after his death are still so relevant today. Rudd comments on Bonhoeffer's dissent of the perversion of the *Two Kingdoms doctrine* which confined the Christian gospel to the inner person, the sphere where the Kingdom of God reigns and the Kingdom of the State which is not subject to the gospel's message—a dichotomy which led the German people to support and commit to some of the most awful atrocities toward fellow human beings. Rudd points out that Bonhoeffer in his seminal work asks the question, "What is Meant By Telling the Truth?[234] This question represented a call to the German Church to assume a prophetic role in speaking out in defence of the defenceless in the face of a hostile state. Rudd says further:

> For Bonhoeffer, "Obedience to God's will, may be a religious experience but it is not an ethical one until it issues in actions that can be socially valued." He railed at a Church for whom Christianity was "a metaphysical abstraction to be spoken of only at the edges of life," and in which clergy blackmailed their people with hellish consequences for those whose sins the clergy were adept at sniffing out, all the while ignoring the real evil

beyond their cathedrals and churches. "The Church stands," he argued, "not at the boundaries where human powers give out, but in the middle of the village . . . ." Bonhoeffer's political theology is therefore one of a dissenting church that speaks truth to the state, and does so by giving voice to the voiceless. Its domain is the village (the community) not the interior of the chapel. Its core principle is to stand in defence of the defenceless or . . . those who are "below." Bonhoeffer . . . urged the church . . . to protect the state from itself.[235]

Rudd sees the Church, in its engagement with the state in its social, economic and security policy, speaking directly to the state to give power to the powerless, voice to those who have none, and to point to the great silence in our national discourse where otherwise there are no natural advocates. He challenges the position that there could be truth in politics where compromise is the primary end of the political process. And he calls on the church to speak truthfully, prophetically and incisively in defiance of the superficiality of formal debate in contemporary Western politics. He questions the church as to who is speaking on behalf of our planet? " . . . the fundamental ethical dilemma of our age (is) to protect the planet—in the language of the Bible, to be proper stewards of creation."[236] Regarding the challenge of global poverty, he asks:

> , . . . who speaks boldly to the state for those who cannot speak for themselves? Today, 1.4 billion people live below the poverty line defined by the World Bank of US$1 per day. Who speaks for them? For them, there is a great and continuing silence. In the absence of total catastrophe, they cannot capture the television sets of our collective imagination. They are, in part, victims of the great immorality of our age: if it's not on the six o'clock news, it's not happening. The UN's Millennium Development Goals represent a partial response to this. The failure to give effect to those goals represents continued ethical failure— . . . where lip-service, not moral leadership, is the order of the day.[237]

Rudd believes that had Bonhoeffer been alive—a man who was killed for believing that a God of Justice demanded that he believed in and lived out this justice in his every day life—he would be traumatized by the privatized, pietised and politically compliant Christianity of our day. *"Bonhoeffer's vision of Christianity and politics was for a just world delivered by social action, driven by person[s of] faith."*[238]

I believe that it is important, however, to heed the warning of Doug Bandow:

> [that while] religion and politics do go together . . . their partnership should emphasize transcendent principles rather than specific policies. The relationship . . . should never be a comfortable one . . . the state . . . ordained by God . . . is a temporary, worldly institution run by sinful man . . . ; the promise of the Kingdom of God is quite different . . . ; the Christian political activist must never forget that God, not the state, will ultimately bring about His Kingdom. [239]

Jim Wallis, a public theologian, Christian activist and prolific writer, in his passionate book, *The Soul of Politics,* categorically points out that "the world isn't working . . . ; the depth of the crisis we face demands more than politics as usual". [240] He goes on to comment regarding his country, the United States:

> An illness of the spirit has spread across the land, and our greatest need is for what our religious traditions call "the healing of the nations" . . . ; the fundamental character of the social, economic, and cultural renewal we urgently need will require a change of both our hearts and our minds. But that change will demand a new kind of politics—a politics with spiritual values. [241]

He calls for a new political vision with real moral values. For him both liberalism and conservatism have run their course and have outlived their usefulness. He admits that neither liberal sociology nor conservative piety has any impact on the deeply entrenched evils of the day. As he sees it most of the social, economic and political issues that confront our world are spiritual at its core.[242]

Wallis' strong appeal is for a politics that offers a vision of transformation, "a politics of meaning", "a politics of faith", because it is only to such would "a politics of power" yield to usher in a "politics of community." [243]

A very similar cry goes forth from the Caribbean region. Caribbean societies built on the notion of social exclusion in education, health care, justice and other institutions are voicing increasing demands for a politics of community, a politics of inclusion. Reverend Garnett Roper calls on the Christian church, the community of Christ, to offer leadership in this new vision. Our life of faith and our commitment to Jesus Christ provide the basis for our vision of hope and acts of love. Roper as he studies Scripture notes, "the realities which overwhelm . . . people in the Caribbean . . . are not beyond the grace and mercy of God in Jesus Christ. He has responded to them and laid a blueprint which offers liberating and transforming options for us. "[244]

Jim Wallis articulates an alternative which he posits as "prophetic spirituality" which is rooted in the prophetic biblical tradition of the Hebrew sages, Jesus Christ and the early church community. It is the movement which has under-pinned, every renewal and reform movement in history that has sought to return to radical religious roots . . . ; It relates biblical faith to social transformation; personal conversion to the cry of the poor . . . core religious values to new economic priorities . . . the call of community to racial and gender justice . . . spirituality to politics . . . . The politics we most need right now is the "politics of community.[245]

The question we may wish to ask at this point is, "Who in the Caribbean Region will lead this process of change? What manner of leadership would be prepared to pay the costly price of serving in faith, hope and love?

THE CALLING OF LEADERSHIP

"The Caribbean needs moral leadership," so says Grenada's Prime Minister, the Honourable Tillman Thomas in a press commentary on the local and regional crime situation today. Even as I write (May 2010), our airways are bombarded with news coming out of Jamaica, a Caribbean nation now

under siege by criminal elements who are not prepared to respond to the tenets and dictates of law and order. For decades, Jamaica has witnessed the development of what are described as "garrison communities," often alleged to be aligned to rival political sides with strong partisan loyalties. The problems which today have brought Jamaica to such a frightening level of civil disruption and human destruction (dozens of 'innocent' persons are reported dead) are certainly not unique to Jamaica.

The rest of the English speaking Caribbean facing similar problems—poverty, unemployment, crime, social exclusion and social and economic injustice, racial rivalries, political tribalism, family disintegration and violence, youth alienation, community decadence, political corruption and incompetence, moral bankruptcy and spiritual apathy—is poised to suffer similar violent implosion and defiance by criminal elements who have been allowed to become more and more powerful, while "good" people sermonize, moralize and philosophize.

In speaking with a close friend, a Jamaican, about what is happening in her beloved homeland, she yearns that as a people they would not shelve the *process* because of the *pain* that is involved in real change. She confesses that 'good' people have felt powerless and have given over power to 'bad' people. It is her view that people of faith may have to be prepared to give their lives to 'save' her country. Indeed, her heart's cry is for strong, moral leadership, risky leadership, leaders of faith—leaders who are both called and chosen. [246]

In exploring what I have termed, the *Calling of Leadership,* I will draw heavily on some favourite texts as I pull together my own determinations on the vocation of leadership, and how it fits into the challenges of a politics of change within the context of a life of faith. I have read dozens of books on Leadership, and wholeheartedly agree with Robert C. Tucker in his quotation of James MacGregor Burns, who contends that, "Leadership is one of the most observed and least understood phenomena on earth." [247]

Yes, indeed, leadership is one of those concepts that, though given prodigious attention in the readings of the social sciences, and though mandatory in any study of organizations, institutions and societies, remains a mysterious, elusive and un-definable aspect of human relating. Some persons have even given up on the notion. Peter Block who opts for stewardship over leadership, observes:

> It is this pervasive and almost religious belief in leaders that slows the process of genuine reform . . . ; we think the task of leaders is to create an environment where we can live a life of safety and predictability . . . if we were not looking so hard for leadership, others would be unable to claim sovereignty over us. Our search for great bosses is not that we like being watched and directed; it is that we believe that clear authority relationships are the antidote to crisis and ultimately the answer to chaos. [248]

Traditionally, leadership has been defined on the basis of history, traits, environment, behaviour of leaders, relationship of leaders and followers. It is not my intent to go into these; the literature abounds on the various approaches to leadership. I would surmise that each approach offers some light but each alone is incomplete.

My focus in this short discourse is to bring together thoughts which I deem to have been most instructive in my incursion into the study of leadership and which may have had the most impact on my own leadership journey. My hope is that these thoughts and reflections will add to the ongoing conversation on the search for leadership which is urgently required in the Caribbean at this time, as we complete the first decade of the twenty-first century.

We are all leaders. As humans, we are all called to lead, to influence, to be civil, to be righteous, and to do the right thing. Others look on us; we look to others for direction and counsel. We lead in some sphere of our lives—at home among family, at school among peers, at the workplace among colleagues, in the community among neighbours and villagers, in the church among brethren and sistren, in the society among comrades and friends. It is an intensely human enterprise and does not fit neatly into any paradigm or category. And that is why if I had to select a definition of leadership from among the hundreds of definitions proffered I would agree with Blaine Lee when he states leadership is about being a person;

"it is a journey toward integrity, union and wholeness. It is a journey that starts on the inside!"[249]

This type of leadership is more about character (who you are) than about competence (what you do). Stephen Covey calls it, *Principle—Centered Leadership*; [250] Blaine Lee terms it, *Leadership with Honor*, [251] M. Scott Peck describes it as *Leadership as Vocation*,[252] Robert K. Green-leaf commends it as *Servant Leadership*.[253] All of these visions offer a transcendence to leadership that when omitted is more death producing than life affirming; it is about *being* as well as doing.

I noted in Part Two of this work an important observation of Stephen Covey that the fundamental nature of the problems we face today could not easily be solved at the superficial level at which they were created. The problems of our region cannot be tackled with more of the same. We need a shift in our paradigm on how politics is done; we need a perspective transformation on the meaning of democracy; we need civility in our parliaments and participation in our communities; we need conversion among our leaders. We need leaders who will see politics as vocation not profession; as a covenantal relationship with God through faith, not merely a means of gaining personal status and power, privilege and control.

Leadership as vocation is what Scott Peck sees as civility—a commodity that is sadly lacking in our world and our leaders today. He sees the notion of civility operating wherever there is a relationship between two or more people and thus he defines civility as consciously motivated organizational behaviour. It is the intentional act of becoming more conscious of ourselves, others and the organizations in which we relate. [254]

Scott Peck elaborates on three significant cornerstones of civility: (1) the ethical consciousness of other people, individually and collectively as precious beings (2) the other being the act of seeing human beings as precious because they are created by God and reflect the divine image of their Creator, and (3) that one (the civil leader) must be in a relationship of willing submission to God, Creator.[255] These elements of civility must constitute the basis of our leadership covenant.

How can this essence of civility be brought into our politics? Is it possible? I ask with so many others who are yearning for change. The cry can be heard from east to west, north to south, popes and presidents, community activists and university scholars. President Barack Obama during the height of the debate over the deeply controversial and divisive Health Care Bill (2009/10) called openly for more *civility* in Washington. [256] In the recent national election processes in Grenada (2008), Antigua and Barbuda (2009) and Trinidad and Tobago (2010) the calls for change in our politics resounded.

As I continue to explore the *being of* leadership, permit me to include a story, more accurately, a parable, from the Judeo-Christian Bible found in Matthew, Chapter 22, verses 1—14, and entitled, "The Parable of the Wedding Banquet" or "The Marriage of the King's Son." Jesus told His listeners the story of a King who invited many to the marriage of his son—the initial invitees were all too busy and refused the invitation, some quite violently. The King then ordered that the invitation be opened to all and sundry—*good and bad.* This was done. The King while greeting his guests discovered that among those who had accepted the invitation was one who was not wearing the required wedding robe or appropriate garment. The King immediately ordered that she be thrown out. You see, "The garment represents an absolute requirement for entrance . . . the robe of imputed righteousness that God graciously provides to man through faith"[257] There was a requirement for entrance and no one was acceptable who did not meet that criteria. Jesus in telling this parable cryptically concluded with the statement, *"*For many are called, but few are chosen*".* (Matthew 22:14 KJV).

Today, the calling to leadership is open to all; the 'choseness' for leadership is met by few. All around is heard, *"there is a crisis in leadership;" "the world is experiencing a leadership crisis."* Very often we are not sure to exactly what we allude—stronger leaders, visionary leaders, honest leaders, un-corruptible leaders, compassionate leaders, participatory leaders—perhaps all this and more. We know, however, at the depths of our souls that something is missing. Something is wrong in our world. And with every new promise of change our hopes are dashed to pieces on the shores of disappointment, frustration and despair.

Today our world is experiencing a dearth and death of "chosen" leaders. Our leadership crisis is not for a lack of leaders; our tragedy is that there are so few "chosen" leaders—men and women of faith, women and men of faith. There is a general call to leadership but only the *faith-full* ones are chosen and these are few. Our governments and parliaments are peopled with leaders who have failed to put on the required garment. Myles Munroe, Caribbean writer, deplores the lack of "true leadership" throughout the world and describes the majority of current leaders as *pseudoleaders.*[258]

"Chosen" leadership is a choice; a hard choice; actually a dangerous choice, but the only choice that offers us an opportunity to further God's plan of wellbeing for His beloved world. But, you may ask, what does this 'chosen' leader look like? Having opted for faith and meaning and purpose; having chosen the path of obedience to God Who is Supreme in all things, what would such leadership look like? Permit me to present a portrait of what "chosen" leadership would look like. It is by no means a complete work. Indeed the vision has just started with me, and my strokes would be rather broad, sometimes blurry. An invitation is open to all who would like to join the wedding banquet—sumptuous robes are ready which may sometimes feel like 'hair-shirts.' But remember leadership is an often painful journey into meaning and integrity, and that's what *faith* is also about.

Having scouted the leadership literature, I have rather boldly selected seven aspects of a vision of leadership which, to me, closely approximate the "Chosen" leader or faith-filled leader; they are: Chief of Sinners, Servant Leader, Team Player, Peace Maker, Change Agent, Culture Builder, and Power Sharer. I will now spend some time elaborating on each of these aspects of leadership.

I have elected to begin with the portrait of *Chief of Sinners* and this is because it is perhaps the most difficult and least used acts of modern day leadership, but herein lies the making or breaking of "chosen" leadership. The Apostle Paul, first century Christian martyr, one of the greatest leaders of all times, whose writings continue over the past two millennia to guide the thinking and impact the lives of millions of people confessed that he was the "chief of sinners."

The Judeo-Christian Scriptures record in First Timothy, Chapter One, Paul's statement: "Here's a word you can take to heart and depend on: Jesus Christ came into the world to save sinners. I'm proof—**Public Sinner Number One**—someone who could never had made it apart from sheer mercy. And now He shows me off—every evidence of His endless patience—to those who are right on the edge of trusting Him forever" (1 Timothy:1:15, 16, MSG. emphasis mine)

Of all the several books I have read on leadership, I count Dan Allender's *Leading with a Limp* to be among the most powerful and insightful. I owe Dr. Allender for this vision of "Chief of Sinners," which describes his graphic and persuasive portrayal of the "reluctant leader" or the "limping leader." Within the first pages of his book, he makes the following point: "This is the strange paradox of leading: to the degree you attempt to hide or dissemble your weaknesses, the more you will need to control those you lead, the more insecure you will become, and the more rigidity you will impose . . . ; The dark spiral of spin control inevitably leads to people's cynicism and mistrust."[259]

Allender, who draws on his own experiences as a leader, is not simply calling for an expedient acknowledgement of one's shortcomings, particularly, when one is caught, but an intentional openness to one's imperfections noting that when Paul, the Apostle confessed that he was a chief sinner, he was doing so in a letter to his young, spiritual son Timothy, and of course, to the young church with whom the letter would be shared. Paul knew from his experience with God that "you are the strongest when you are weak, and you are the most courageous when you are broken. You find your greatest effectiveness as a leader when you lead with a distinct limp."[260]

Biblical leaders like Moses, Jeremiah, Jonah and others seem to indicate that God appears to choose leaders who don't want to lead. God knows, of course, the narcissism which characterizes the human heart and seeks to find persons who are not easily seduced by power, pride and ambition. The "chief of sinners," leader with a limp, strikes a blow at the deadly enemy of pride which is the perverted type of self-worship found in so many of our leaders today.[261] Too many leaders in our region who start off well, with some years into governing descend into a type of narcissism that breeds a culture of idolatry and dependency among those around them, destroying any goodness that may have existed. Too many of our current leaders have succumbed to the deadly snare of pride and take the nation with them.

Leaders with a limp, chief of sinners choose honesty over "spin." Tragically "spin" has become a hallmark of the region's politics. The more brilliant the 'spin-doctor', the louder he or she is hailed as a great politician! How far we have gone in twisting truth and substituting lies for truth! Allender puts it this way:

> A community of good characters must tell honest and compelling stories in order to become a transformative community. Unfortunately, what most organizations offer instead of good stories is spin. Stories have the power to shape character; spin is a story without soul or suffering, a story which consequently creates hypocrisy. Spin is of the devil.[262]

We have become leaders who major in spin, and politics have become disreputable and politicians untrustworthy.

It would certainly be spin to present "chief of sinners" leadership as if it carried no cost.

It is risky, often painful and lonely, and charged with complexities and times of chaos and crisis. Being intentional, honest and open may lead to loss of respect and loss of influence, including 'loss of power' or removal from office. In-spite of these risks, however, speaking the truth, though frightening, "invites others—by the Spirit's prompting—to look more honestly at their own need for forgiveness, freedom, and courage. It also removes the dividing wall of hierarchy and false assumptions about people in power and gives the leader who humbles himself the opportunity to be lifted up by God"[263]

The Caribbean urgently needs today, women and men of courage and faith, "chief of sinners" leadership!

Having confessed as "chief of sinners," a leader can now commit to a life of *servant leadership*. This type of leadership has been popularized by Robert Greenleaf in his seminal work on *Servant Leadership* widely acclaimed in the organizational arena, and profusely used in political rhetoric. Ron Boehme, public theologian, as he critically assessed the state of the world at the end of the twentieth century, identified the waning of 400 years of civilization in the West, the decay of the Western culture with a concomitant vacuum in leadership, a desperate search to advance global community including freedom and democracy, the advent of a powerful and pervasive Information Age, the failure of secular materialistic humanism as the religion of the West, and noted the emergence of a new trend. For him this trend is a positive one as he envisions whole nations changed and established in strength through the means of servant leadership.[264]

Servant leadership as defined by Greenleaf is strong natural leadership which begins with the natural feeling of being of service moving to a conscious aspiration to lead. The motivation that drives behaviour is servant-hood.[265] It is all about character, not style or status. The servant leader can take on or give up a position of power without losing the servant nature. President Jimmy Carter is identified as one such leader who having moved from the presidency took on the task of building homes for those who could not afford them through Habitat for Humanity. A servant leader is compassionate, caring, accountable, willing to listen, willing to share power and willing to admit flaws and failures. Robert Greenleaf sought to show that the traditional role of leaders as bosses was no longer effective or acceptable but that people were crying out for trusted leaders and would respond only to those who have proved themselves to be such.
[266]

I agree wholeheartedly with Greenleaf's proposition of the ultimate effectiveness and desperate search for servant leadership in today's world and would add that men and women may have accepted the calling to lead from a view point of self-interest, and may find themselves having to choose service over self-interest in response to the demand for more trustworthy and mature leadership. This shift in approach is usually accompanied and underpinned by a growing faith commitment. Most, or should I say all of the leaders whom I would carefully categorize as servant leaders, some of whom I have mentioned in this book, have been persons who have experienced seasons of doubt, brokenness and pain and who have come to what is described as a *religious conversion* concerned with relationship to God, a *moral conversion* concerned with interpersonal relationships, and a *political conversion* concerned with a commitment to justice. All three commitments are reflected in the prophetic words of the prophet Micah of the Judeo Christian Scripture: "*He has showed you O man, what is good. And what does the Lord require of you?* **To act justly, to love mercy and to walk humbly with your God**" [emphasis mine]. (Micah 6:8).

This is the essence of servant Leadership! This is the leadership I wish to propose—redeemed servant leadership! Redeemed by the grace and mercy of God!

Tom Marshall in his book, *Understanding Leadership* noted that Jesus Christ not only redeemed power but He also created and modelled a new kind of leadership to handle redeemed power. Indeed he stresses that the only kind of leader that can be safely entrusted with power without being corrupted with the power is the servant leader who gets his mandate from the One true leader, Jesus Christ.[267] The Biblical worldview provides us with the gospel account of Jesus as He poignantly modelled servant leadership to his closest friends and disciples. It was the night before His crucifixion—the night before He paid with His life to redeem humanity and everything else that defined our humanness, leadership, power, faith — He took off His outer robe, put on an apron and washed the dirty, smelly feet of His disciples. Jesus turned the world's values upside down. He started a revolution in relationships—the leader as servant. He redefined leadership. And lest they forgot that powerful act, His words to them were: "Now that I Your Lord and Teacher have washed your feet,, you also should wash one another's feet. I leave you an example that you should do as I have done" (John 13:14-15, NIV). Permit me to state confidently that this is the only type of leadership that can restore a dying humanity. The challenge today is to accept God's gift of redemption in Christ Jesus by faith and to humbly (before God) and meekly (with each other) serve as chosen leaders—leaders who having being called are prepared, with others, to choose the thorny path of service and the complex life of faith.

This kind of path to service and life of faith can seldom be journeyed alone. A servant leader is not a lone ranger or a maximum leader. A servant leader is a team worker; some would say a team-player. As Gene Wilkes sees it, "Leadership of a team is the highest expressions of servant leadership."[268] He describes team leadership as embodying the very principles which underlie servant leadership, humility rather than pride, cooperation instead of rivalry, valuing empowerment over control.[269] The values of team leadership are clearly antithetical to modern day political leadership. The virtues and values of team work is widely extolled today but seldom practiced. I do not think that I need make a case for team work. We tend to know instinctively that two are better than one, that *a cord of three strands is not quickly broken* (Ecclesiastes 4:12, NIV). If the value of teamwork is so obvious in its advantages, the question may then be asked, "why do leaders so seldom chose team-building over individualistic-achieving?"

Only biblical theism provides an adequate answer to that question. A biblical worldview recognizes man's sinful bent to self-centeredness and self-aggrandizement. Biblical theism records a history of man's alienation from God, self and others. A team spirit cannot thrive where there is alienation and distrust. It takes a "chosen" leader to seek the pain-filled path of reconciliation and the heart-breaking choice of trust. A "chosen" leader understands the imperative for this team spirit and spends himself or herself in fostering this spirit. This spirit thrives best when it is based on faith in a faithful Godhead. A faith-filled leader sees team-building as a priority. Team-building like community-making is an intentional, dynamic experience which involves giving up of self—centered agendas and hidden motivations, and moving to increasingly embrace openness, other-centeredness and relational mutuality. I dare to say that only "chosen" servant leaders, with a limp, engage in this "crisis of choice" and opt to take the more difficult, but infinitely more, healthy way of leadership. So powerful is this process that biblical history records where God personally intervened to disrupt the work of a group of people who were working *together* against their Creator to build what was described as the Tower of Babel—a monument to their own strength and power. "But the Lord came down to see the city and the tower that the men were building. The Lord said, "If as one people speaking the same language they have begun to do this, then nothing they plan to do will be impossible for them" (Genesis 11:5-7 NIV). The Sovereign Godhead knew the power of teamwork. Would to God that leaders of the Caribbean region would grasp a hold of this vision and run with it from Bahamas in the North to Guyana in the South! What a difference it would make in our region!

Even now, in the closing of the first decade of the twenty first century, Parliamentarians of the Eastern Caribbean are debating what is called, *Treaty Establishing The Organization of Eastern Caribbean States Economic Union*. This treaty envisages a widening and deepening of the integration process in nine small island states. This is indeed a laudable and much needed initiative in order to battle with the global realities of our time and to strengthen our regional resource-base. There is need for a special commitment to humble, serving, team-builders if this process is to bring the quality of life that our region seeks. It is my hope and prayer that more and more "chosen" leaders would emerge to guide, direct and strengthen this community of people who are shackled by our past history, our present in-competencies, hope-less methodologies and unsustainable strategies.

Working together brings peace! Scott Peck identified that peace is one of the recognizable characteristics of community. [270] The Prince of Peace, Jesus Christ, exhorts: *"You're blessed when you can show people how to cooperate instead of compete or fight. (*a peace-maker). *That's when you discover who you really are and your place in God's family"* (Matthew 5:9, MSG).

As I noted earlier in my discussion on peace-making, peace is an indispensable condition for economic and social development. Wars divert energies and resources and large scale poverty and unemployment and social injustice undermine any attempt at peaceful living.

The painful and alarming divisions between races, classes, gender, religion, ethnicity, generations and other such, which confront our world make peace an increasingly elusive goal. We dare not give up, however. Peace is indeed both the pre-requisite to and consequence of developing our communities and nations. Today, in the Caribbean millions and millions of dollars are spent on national security in attempting to keep our region as a zone of peace. Resources that are needed for education, health and social development are pumped into purchasing military equipment for our special forces to keep our countries safe. And of course, it would be naïve to expect a violence—or crime-free world. But crime and violence are escalating.

The Caribbean is a seething cauldron of crime and a hotbed of violence, in comparison to our size. Criminals are becoming bolder and crimes increasingly vicious. Tragically too, crime and violence are now linked to politics, with politicians alleged to be the providers or supporting the provision of ammunition to party 'faithfulls' for protection.

The Caribbean is looking for leadership who can be characterized as peace-makers in order to stop the dangerous drift towards violent and crime-ridden societies. The Caribbean needs "chosen" leaders—persons of peace, gentle as doves but wise as serpents. The Caribbean urgently needs leaders who are not afraid of struggle which may sometimes be physical, but who will always seek a way of dialogue, of engagement, of creative management and resolution of conflicts.

The leaders of peace must, however, never forget that we are engaged in a gigantic *spiritual* warfare—indeed in a conflict of the Kingdoms (the Kingdom of evil against the Kingdom of God), and that spiritual resistance is absolutely necessary in this arena of struggle. Such leaders who are persons of *faith* recognize that the fight "is not against flesh and blood, but against the rulers, against the authorities, against the powers of this dark world and against the spiritual forces of evil in the heavenly realms"(Ephesians 6:12 NIV). They know without a doubt that the most effective weapon of defence and offense is the power of God. The leader who is a peacemaker has made his or her peace with God and enjoys the peace of God and accepts the indispensible need to practice spiritual disciplines such as bible study, prayer and worship. The leader of peace accepts by faith that God is both the Source and Sustainer of peace and that ultimate peace will come from Him and with Him. In the meantime, the Leader, peacemaker is mandated to plant seeds of peace, to courageously and creatively go forth to engage in peace-making initiatives, to support and use non-violent ways of dealing with conflict as much as possible, to commit to be an ambassador of reconciliation and a dispenser of goodwill and respect toward all God's creatures and creation.

The Leader, peacemaker is a change agent! Lasting change begins at the personal level with the man or woman in the mirror. To be an agent of change, the "chosen" leader begins with herself. As Blaine Lee sees it, when we change the principles we live by, we will change the world.[271] He went on to note, 'The need for change in the world is great . . . but to change the world we must start with ourselves. Gandhi challenged us to become the change we seek in the world." [101] Lee also reminds his readers of the powerful statement of Max DePree: "*We cannot become what we need to be by remaining what we are.*"[272]

Stephen Covey describes it as almost axiomatic to say that personal change must precede organizational change.[273] Herein lay, however, our greatest tragedy in the Caribbean region. Our leaders spend little or no time on personal change. They view it as 'soft' or irrelevant to the task at hand (community and societal change) and dismiss such calls for training in personal development as a waste of time *"that can't win elections."* I can well recall my own frustrated experience as an elected politician and member of cabinet, entreating my colleagues to make available some *quality* time (not just a hit and miss session) for training in issues like teambuilding, values clarification, visioning, conflict-resolution, principled-centered and character-based leadership and other pertinent areas of personal development.

There are increasing calls today, however, for "transformational leadership." But it is significant to note that these calls come primarily from women leaders who have weighed traditional, transactional leadership in the balance and found it to be much wanting. Covey defines transformational leadership as leadership that seeks to change the realities of one's particular world to more nearly conform to values and ideals; while transactional leadership focuses on efficient interaction of changing realities.[274] He is convinced that *"one person can be a change catalyst, a "transformer," in any situation, any organization . . . (the) yeast that can leaven an entire loaf. It requires vision, initiative, patience, respect, persistence, courage and **faith** to be a transforming leader"*[275] (emphasis mine).

A "chosen" leader as change-agent focuses on change in himself/herself first and prepares himself/ herself for the task of tackling community, organizational and societal change. Our leaders today spend too little time in preparing themselves for the deeply 'spiritual' task of real change. Technical competence though important, is not enough; professional competence though necessary is simply not sufficient to deal with the challenging and complex situations facing mankind today. There is need for a deep inner spirituality, which I believe, receives its reality and comes from faith in a Personal, Infinite God Who is not silent.

Permit me to conclude this very brief exploration in presenting a three-part personal change process which is offered by Blaine Lee as he discusses influencing with honour. We, Caribbean politicians, are big on the title of "Honourable". I would highly recommend the reading of Blaine Lee's book, where he points out that honor is not something that is simply conferred; indeed it is earned. He talks of creative, not destructive and manipulative use of power. Honor is power, the kind of power that is genuine and lasting and it is not the type that comes with a position; it is neither quick nor easy; it is a lifelong process.[276] Blaine Lee puts it so well that I'd like to quote him fully:

> Personal change is a three-part process that requires giving up old views and behaviors, considering new possibilities, and then stabilizing new ways. It consists of challenging old ideas, gaining awareness, experiencing hope, trying new ways by doing something new that is congruent with what we really want. But it is not neatly linear. In the real world it is messy and there are detours and sometimes your heart breaks and you get lost. It takes time. It can be discouraging. It takes commitment and persistence. It will require patience. And it's like cultivating a beautiful flower; you can't plug one in; you have to grow it and tend to it, and protect it and nurture it. For a while it is fragile. But it is a work of art, and it will benefit all who see it.[277]

The leader who is a change agent begins with herself. There are no shortcuts. Ask some of our greatest leaders how they did it and they will tell their story. Ask Nelson Mandela, one of our leaders of honour today and you will hear him poignantly share:

> I have walked that long road to freedom. I have tried not to falter; I have made missteps along the way. I have discovered

the secret that after climbing a great hill, one finds that there are many more hills to climb. I have taken a moment here to rest, to steal a view of the glorious vista that surrounds me, to look back on the distance I have come. But I can rest only for a moment, for with freedom comes responsibilities, and I dare not linger, for my long walk is not yet ended.[278]

"Chosen" leaders of honour impact their culture. Indeed, they are culture-builders. For many decades Caribbean peoples have debated over the idea of culture. Do we have a Caribbean culture? What is it? How is it defined? Often when we think of culture or even allude to it, we think of popular entertainment, festivals, the arts, etc. And although some of our most eminent Caribbean writers such as George Lamming, Rex Nettleford and others have written of and explicated on a much wider understanding of culture, in significant ways, we continue to see culture as said to have been described by Lamming as *the icing on the cake* rather than *the very cake we are making*.[279]

As I explore the task of culture-building in leadership, I'd like to use Lamming's broad definition of culture as the way we define and present ourselves—a way which allows us to use what he describes as the *sovereignty of the imagination*.[280] If culture is perceived in this way and not as something handed down to us by colonizing powers (both political and intellectual) over which we have no control, then we can indeed be culture-makers.

Ron Boehme boldly asserts:

> Creating culture is what man was placed on earth to do. God gave man the mandate to tend, rule and cultivate the earth . . . God expected man to make the earth a place for the glory and worship of Him. Man was not meant to fill the world with idolatry and cause his own destruction . . . . Since the coming of Christ to redeem fallen man, this mandate has been given the new meaning of bringing all things under the subjection of Jesus.[281]

He also sees the real battle among the various nations of the earth as the battle for culture, because culture makes a nation, and culture is essentially religious—that which we worship.[282] Boehme shares with his readers Ray Sutton's definition of culture:

"Culture comes from_cultus_meaning worship. Thus (we are) to transform the world into a place of worship, and thereby create true culture . . . . (We are) making society into a proper place to worship God. "[283]

I like that definition! A biblical worldview propounds that creating culture was what the human was placed on this earth to do. "Man was given the unique privilege of taking an entire planet and transforming it into a habitation of fellowship with the living God."[284]

Darrow L. Miller who writes much about worldview and culture, elaborates on humankind's tasks as "culture makers," reflecting the "three faces of culture"—truth, justice and beauty — and resulting in "life, health and development."[285] The importance of this elaboration to Caribbean leaders requires no elucidation. Today, the priority vision as articulated by our leaders, in words if not always in deeds, is the pursuit of the well-being that comes with a preservation of life, promotion of health and pursuit of development. A "chosen" leader warmly embraces the role and responsibility of culture-making. She humbly accepts the fundamental truth that *"human culture was originally designed to express the beauty and reality of God in all His facets and splendor."* [286] A chosen leader repentantly admits that man sinned and with separation from God, the deterioration of culture began. Alas, the story did not end there. The Supreme Godhead began a work of redemption, and through God's only begotten Son, Jesus Christ, the long process of restoration began. In Christ's own words, the mandate went out to all people of faith to be *"the salt of the earth* (and) *light of the world"* (Matthew 5: 13,14 KJV). For those who take these words seriously, it means penetrating our cultures with the love of God and enlightening our cultures with the truth of God.

A "chosen" leader understands that culture is primarily shaped by the worldview of a people and that various worldviews carry with them varying consequences. Indeed, varying worldviews *inevitably* produce different results. And therefore the choice of worldview that underpins one's culture is crucial. And furthermore, the leader has an ongoing responsibility to examine the foundational premises of the nation's culture.

Because culture is not neutral, we can indeed critique our culture. We can distinguish between those things that promote corrupt practice or just action, economic greed or economic well being, creativity or depravity in entertainment, idolatry of the good gifts of God or worship of the One True God.

We can also determine the impact of humanism and secularism on culture. Humanism and secularism say that all cultures are relative and equal. Biblical theism says that some cultures are more mature and righteous than others to the extent that they reflect the values and truth of the Sovereign God of history and culture. The priority challenge of the "chosen" leader is to ensure that the primary foundation of the nation's culture is truly transformative—based on "true" truth, clear absolutes, while its secondary expressions reflect both unity and diversity, morality and maturity. "Chosen" men and women of the Caribbean hear the clear call of God to be culture builders and with the spectacles of truth, a vision of transformation and eyes of faith go forth, often in fear and trembling, with courage and consideration, with character and competence to live *truth*, to promote *justice* and to create *beauty* for the well-being of those served.

Perhaps, among the most difficult of all challenges of "chosen" leadership is the call to be power-sharers. I began with a tough one, *chief of sinners*, and I conclude with an equally formidable one, both daring and risky, *power-sharing*. While the chief of sinners leads with a limp, the power-sharer leads from the side. James R. Lucas in a very useful book entitled *Balance of Power* provided me with some of the clearest discussion on the notion of power-sharing. Permit me therefore to begin my brief discussion with Lucas' description of power-sharing:

> Powersharing is a multifaceted, ongoing exercise that is the essence of true leadership. It's a critical element of . . . success. And it is very hard to do well . . . (it) is releasing the creative and productive capabilities of people . . . in part a process of sharing our power, and in part a decision to use our power in a more expansive, abundant and generous way.[287]

Lucas views cultures of *dependence* (a shortage of power) and cultures of *independence* (an excess of power) as killers of power-sharing and submits that only in *interdependence* can true power-sharing bloom and blossom and that values like *initiative* and *collaboration*—key elements of power-sharing are perverted in both dependent and independent cultures. In dependent cultures initiative means asking for permission to act and collaboration means working with the system; in independent cultures initiative means looking out for number one and collaboration means personal networking.[288] He affirms that initiative and collaboration are best cultivated in interdependent cultures, and introduces the creating of interdependence in these words:

> Building interdependence is a little like weaving a tapestry; there is a beautiful end result, but the work is meticulous and at times, tedious. It's easy to stop before it's finished. And one destructively powerful person or group of people can break with the design pattern and destroy the end result . . . ; Interdependent (nations) are long-term projects. They're hard to build and even harder to maintain . . . ; as human beings and as a culture . . . in our shortsightedness, we use our power to get only what we can see today and reap tomorrow. [289]

I find the above comments to be particularly useful as I consider the historical and present day moments of regional integration in the Caribbean—a movement from dependence through independence to interdependence. This movement is indeed the awesome challenge facing the "chosen" leaders of the Caribbean—the vision of power-sharing within a context of regional interdependence. For the past fifty years or more, Caribbean leaders have been perplexed by the question of "how do we move to the next stage when we are more often than not trapped in a stage of "half-ripe" independence?" Our nations could be described as a mixture of recovering dependencies and struggling independents. Yet we are cautioned in the literature that interdependence is a *choice* that only independent persons can make. No doubt, we have made some significant strides and we owe much to those of our leaders who, in-spite of the utmost challenges, have held on to the vision. But today, the crises of the times are catching up with us and demanding of us increasing maturity and stronger movements toward the process of interdependence.

David Hinds in an extremely insightful discourse on the state of democracy and governance in the Anglophone Caribbean, captures the agonizing of past and present Caribbean leaders as they wrestle with the issue of power-sharing as a way of deepening parliamentary democracy both at the local and regional levels and creating more healthy democratic processes.[290] Hinds shares the strong support for power-sharing of past Caribbean leaders like George Odlum and Tim Hector and present leaders as Parnell Campbell and Basdeo Panday who view such a step as crucial to removing the existing disenfranchisement and disempowerment of the majority of Caribbean peoples.[291]

The Caribbean urgently requires a new generation of power-sharers who come with a full understanding of the perils and pitfalls of power, who have spent quality time dealing with his or her own addiction to power and commits to a continuation of that process.

Our region yearns for risk-taking power-sharers who are prepared to bring more and more of the regions' people into a participatory, democratic process and who recognize the spirituality of power and accept the true source of transcendent power — God, Almighty and Omnipotent. Such are the "chosen" sharers of power needed for "a time such as this"!

Permit me to conclude this rough sketch of a portrait of "chosen" leadership by saying that it is not my intent to present this as the grand solution to the complexity of leadership, the contradictions of politics and the challenges of our small region. The above aspects of "chosen" leadership are offered as a group of indispensables required in the ongoing struggle in leading a process of transformational change in our region. Both the strengths and limitations of each aspect must be carefully considered and critiqued, and accorded its place of usefulness in a vision of change. It is my bold submission, however, that the urgent cries for a politics of change in the Caribbean will find their most creative and transforming response through the being and doing of "chosen" leadership worked out in a commitment to a life of faith.

Joan M. Purcell

THE CENTRALITY OF FAITH: FAITH, POLITICS, LEADERSHIP—THE GREATEST OF THESE IS FAITH

"Without faith it is impossible to please God" (Hebrews 11:6 NIV). Without faith, politics is empty; leadership is shallow; community is impossible; survival is unlikely and chaos is inevitable. The present state of planet earth attests to humanity's vainglorious attempts to reach its destiny without *faith*.

I have attempted a road less travelled in these pages. Indeed in our twenty-first century world it is not politically correct to venture into the domain of the religious, especially biblical theism, as it relates to socio-political change. A post-modern world has debunked all spirituality, especially biblical spirituality. And it is precisely because of the spiritual devastation and moral destruction experienced by our world of the twenty-first century that people are now desperately looking for answers. Is there faith still left on earth?

I say yes! Indeed, I follow with the strong assertion that the leaders of the past and present who have made the most transformational impact on our modern world were leaders who had a vision for social justice rooted in their religious faith.

I sought to identify and present some of these leaders of the past and present whose faith inspired and compelled them to the front line of the battle for justice, freedom, community and peace. As the devastation and destruction accelerate, however, the need has become crucial for an increasing emergence of what Curtiss Paul DeYoung describes as *"mystic-activists."*[292] DeYoung identifies "mystic-activists" as "leaders whose activism consumes them yet is deeply rooted in their faith and in the mystery of the divine. Their activism compels them to reach passionately inward toward the divine for sustenance, wisdom, perseverance, and belonging. Their outward activism needs inward mysticism." [293]

He speaks of a faith experienced through a direct relationship with the divine. It is *"a vibrant, alive and engaged faith."*[294] Deyoung enunciates:

> Mystic-activists have a unique power as a result of **their faith**. They disturb "the status quo and traditional tranquility of the power structure". They also "question dominant societal values or ideological principles and the ruling elite's use of power or wealth and frequently achieve a following and through it generate pressure for major social change". **Their faith** repeatedly influences both those who follow and work with them and the forces aligned against them"[295] (emphasis mine).

DeYoung powerfully elucidates his vision of leadership for the twenty-first century which finds a strong echo in my own heart. I wish to quote at some length:

> May the twenty-first century be a time when many more choose mystic-activism and take a journey of faith in the inner regions of the soul and at the outer regions of the society. Twenty-first century mystic-activists can find God at the margins, because that is where the struggle against injustice is most visible. But they will also discover that God lurks in the shadows of the palaces of power and privilege, waiting for activists to dismantle the very structures that lock society into the evil of institutionalized injustice and separation. Their call to activism must be enriched by a faith that leads to a healing of their own scarred identities and those of others in society. Twenty-first century faith-inspired activists need a faith in God that offers a vision of a revolution of the spirit . . . ; they are fully committed. They take risks. Their action is rooted in contemplation. Yet they move forward without needing the assurance of knowing the outcome. They live by faith and they live their faith.[296]

Our region cries out for "mystic-activists, for "chosen leaders", for men and women, women and men, of faith committed to socio-political change in the midst of formidable philosophical, technological, geo-political and economic challenges. While we have identified much that is wrong with us, we have much for which to offer thanksgiving. As Caribbean people we express grateful thanks for our rich diversity of peoples and cultures, our strong heritage of religious faith on which to build a future of hope, and a community of increasingly free people as we put our faith and trust in the Sovereign Maker and Ruler of our region and our world.

I conclude my vision with a powerful affirmation of faith from the Judeo Christian Scriptures as articulated by Eugene Peterson in his contemporary paraphrase of the Bible in *The Message:*

> The fundamental fact of existence is that this trust in God, this faith, is the firm foundation under everything that makes life worth living. It's our handle on what we can't see. The act of faith is what distinguished our ancestors . . . all these pioneers who blazed the way, all these veterans cheering us on . . . ; It means we'd better get on with it. Strip down, start running—and never quit! No extra spiritual fat, no parasitic sins. Keep your eyes on Jesus, who both began and finished this race we're in. Study how he did it. Because he never lost sight of where he was headed—that exhilarating finish in and with God—he could put up with anything along the way: cross, shame, whatever . . . when you find yourselves flagging in your faith, go over that story again . . . that will shoot adrenaline into your souls!(Hebrews 11:1, 12:1-3)

References

1   Joan Purcell, *Memoirs of a Woman in Politics: Spiritual Struggle* (Bloomington, IN: Authorhouse Publishers, 2009).

2   Neville Roche, "Book Review of Joan Purcell's Memoirs", 2009

3   http://www.un.org/esa/sustdev/sids/sidslist.htm, accessed June 3, 2010

4   Garnett Roper, "Caribbean Reading of Mark 5", Presentation CONECAR, Jamaica, 2009

5   Wendy C. Grenade,"Democracy, Governance and Citizenship: A Community-Based Approach," Discussion Paper 2010.

6   Kathy McAfee. *Storm Signals: Structural Adjustment and Development Alternatives in the Caribbean,* Zed Books Ltd. 1991

7   Ibid, 241

8   Christopher De Allie, Paper on "Global Economic Crisis and its Consequences for the Region", 2009

9   Wendy Grenade, Discussion Paper on "Democracy, Government and Citizenship: A Community-based Approach", 2010, 4

10   Garnet Roper, Paper on "Caribbean Reading of Mark 5", CONECAR, 2009, 1

11   UNICEF, "Situation Analysis of Women and Children in the Eastern Caribbean" , 2007, 8

12   Ibid, 8

13   Ibid, 16

14   Ibid, 20

15   Commissioner of Police, Jamaica, Statement on BBC Caribbean Report 10.05.10

16   Flow Television Channel 6, Weekend News Review, Sunday, May 02, 2010.

17   Adel D. Jones & Ena Trotman Jemmott, "Report on Perception of Child Sexual Abuse in the Eastern Caribbean", 2009.

18   Wendy Grenade, Feature Address at 20th Biennual Conference of the Soroptimist International of the Caribbean Network, "Reclaiming Communities through Service", August 2009, 8

19   Christopher Baker, Resurrection Sunday Sermon,, April 2020

20   Patricia Ellis, Conversation on Poverty in the communities, 2009

21   Wendy Grenade, Feature Address Soroptimist International, 2009, 8

22   Darrell W. Johnson,   *Discipleship on the Edge,* Regent College Publishing, Vancouver, British Columbia, 2004, 16

23   Darrow L. Miller, Discipling Nations, The Power of Truth to Transform Cultures, YWAM Publishing, 2001, 17

24   Ibid, 34

25   Ibid, 41

26   Ibid, 41

27   Ibid, 41

28   Ibid, 44

[29] Ibid, 45/46

[30] John Stott, *Issues Facing Christians Today,* Marshall, Morgan & Scott, 1984

[31] UNICEF Situational Analysis 2007

[32] Darrow L. Miller, 60

[33] Food & Agriculture Organization , Paper presented on the Global Food Crisis: Implication for the Developing World, Sept.2009

[34] Myles Munroe, *The Burden of Freedom,* Charisma House, 2000, 134

[35] Ibid, 221

[36] Ibid, 230

[37] Darrow L. Miller, 74

[38] Jim Wallis, *The Soul of Politics; Beyond "Religious Right" and "Secular Left",* Harcourt, Brace & Company, 1995, 176/177

[39] David Hinds, "Beyond Formal Democracy: The Discourse on Democracy and Governance in the Anglophone Caribbean," Commonwealth & Comparative Politics, Volume 46, Issue 3, July 2008

[40] Ibid, 203/4

[41] Darrow L. Miller, *Discipling Nations: The power of Truth to Transform Cultures,* YWAM Publishing, 2001, 49

[42] Richard Foster, *Money, Sex and Power: The Challenge of the Disciplined Life,* Hodder & Stoughton, 1985, 212.

[43] Ibid, 212

[44] Donald Dorr, *Spirituality & Justice,* Orbis Books, New York, 1984, 56

[45] Michael Witter, *Social Change: Christian and Social Science Perspectives,* edited by Mark Figueroa and Judith Soares, Department of Economics, UWI, Jamaica, Monograph # 3, 1987

[46] Carl F. Ellis, *Beyond Liberation: The Gospel of the Black American Experience,* InterVarsity Press, 1983, 20 -23

[47] Rex M. Nettleford, *Caribbean Cultural identity: The Case of Jamaica,* Institute of Jamaica, 1978, x

[48] Wendy Grenade, Feature Address delivered on the 20th Biennual Conference of the Soroptimist International of the Caribbean Network, "Reclaiming Communities through Service", August 2009

[49] Darrow L. Miller, "Culture: Where the Physical & Spiritual Converge", article from forthcoming book on Biblical Theology and Vocation by YWAM Publishing , in 2009 Personal Prayer Diary, YWAM 2009, .20

[50] Ibid, 19

[51] Richard Dawkins, *The God Delusion,* Bantam Press, 2006

[52] Carl F. Ellis, *Beyond Liberation,* 1983, 23

[53] Myles Munroe, *The Burden of Freedom,* Charisma House, 2000, 229.

[54] Ibid, 1

[55] Richard Foster, *Money, Sex and Power: The Challenge of the Disciplined Life,* Hodder and Stoughton, 1985, 196

[56] John R.W.Stott, *Our Social & Sexual Revolution: Major Issues for a New Century,* Baker Books, 1999, 223

57   Darrow L. Miller, *Discipling Nations: The Power of Truth to Transform Cultures,* YWAM Publishing, 2001

58   Ibid, 3

59   ⁵A.R. Bernard, Sunday Sermon, May 03, 2009, Christian Cultural Centre, Brooklyn, NY

60   Dwight Venner, Feature Address at the Launch of a Public Consultation process on the Establishment of the OECS Economic Union, March 2009

61   Peggy Antrobus, Paper on "The Empowerment of Women", WAND, 1989

62   Maxine Henry-Wilson, Paper on "The Poor and the Powerless", 1992, 2

63   President of Guyana, TV Interview on Caribbean News Service, May 25, 2009

64   Government of Grenada, Budget Speech, January 2009

65   George Beckford,& Michael Witter, *Small Garden, Bitter Weeds: Struggle and Change in Jamaica,* Maroon Publishing House, 1982, 61

66   Ibid, 61

67   Elaine Storkey, *What's Right with Feminism,* Eerdmans Publishing Co., 1985, 130

68   Francis Schaeffer, *How Should we then live? The Rise and Decline of Western Thought and Culture,* Crossway Books, 1984, 121

69   Elaine Storkey, 133

70   Lawrence Crabb, Lecture Series, School of Spiritual Direction, Glen Eyrie, Colorado Springs, USA, October 07-10, 2004

Joan M. Purcell

71 Donald Dorr, *Spirituality & Justice,* Orbis Books, NY, 1984, 16 -17

72 Jeremy Rifkin, *Entropy: A New World View,* Viking Press, 1980, 128

73 Ibid, 128

74 Ibid, 129

75 M. Scott Peck, *The Road Less Travelled: A New Psychology of Love, Traditional Values and Spiritual Growth,* Simon & Shuster, NY, 1987, 267

76 Johan Galtung, "Towards a New Economics: on the theory and practice of self-reliance" in *The Living Economy, Edited by Paul Ekins,* Routledge and Kenan Paul, 1986, 100

77 Ibid, 101

78 Ibid, 101

79 Denis Goulet, *Cruel Choice: A New Concept in the Theory of Development,* Atheneum Books, 1973, 328

80 Johan Galtung, 103

81 Manfred Max-Neef, "Human-scale economics: the challenges ahead" in *The Living Economy,* edited by Paul Ekins, Routledge and Kenan Paul, 1986, 44

82 Maxine Henry-Wilson, 1986, 11

83 Francis Schaeffer and Udo W. Middelmann, *Pollution and the Death of Man: The Christian View of Ecology, Good New Publishers,*1992, 45/46

84 Rifkin, 1980, 234/233

85 Ibid, 235

86 Donald Dorr, 1984, 135

87 Richard Foster, *Money, Sex and Power: The Challenge of the Disciplined Life,* Hodder and Stoughton, 1985, 105

88 Ibid, 105

89 Ibid, 72

90 Donald Dorr, 1984, 144

91 Richard Foster, *Celebration of Discipline: The Path to Spiritual Growth,* Harper Collins, 1988, 80

92 International Congress on World Evangelization, "Lausanne Covenant", 1974, 8

93 M. Scott Peck, *The Different Drum: Community Making and Peace,* Simon Schuster, 1987, 17

94 Ibid, 60

95 Ibid, 60

96 Ibid, 61-63

97 Ibid, 65

98 Maddan Handa, Lecture Notes on Peace Education, Ontario Institute for Studies in Education, 1986

99 Joshua Liebman, *Peace of Mind,* Simon & Schuster, 1946, (Out of print)

100 Johan Galtung, *Peace by Peaceful Means: Peace and Conflict, Development and Civilization,* Sage Publications, 1996, 180

101   Ibid, 181

102   Lisa Ostergaard, (ED), *Gender and Development,* Commission of the European Communities, 1992, 6

103   Ibid, 6

104   Errol Miller, *Men at Risk,* Jamaica Publishing House Ltd., 1991, 110

105   Ibid, 115

106   Ibid, 116

107   Peggy Antrobus, *The Global Women's Movement: Issues and Strategies for the New Century,* Zed Books, 2005, 34

108   Errol Miller, 1991, 242

109   Ibid, 281

110   Harvie M. Conn, *Evangelism: Doing Justice and Preaching Grace,* Zondervan, Pub. House, 1962, 95

111   Ibid, 95

112   Myles Munroe, *Burden of Freedom,* Charisma House, 2000, 238

113   Harvie M. Conn, 64

114   Ibid, 64/65

115   Ibid, 67

116   Jim Wallis, *The Soul of Politics: Beyond "Religious Right" and "Secular Left",* Harcourt, Bruce & Company, 1995, 27

117 Stephen Covey, *Seven Habits of Highly Effective People,* Simon & Schuster, 1990, 91/63

118 Charles Colson, *Against the Night: Living in the New Dark Age,* 1989, 67

119 Stephen Covey, *Seven Habits of Highly Effective People,* 65 -94

120 Ibid, 95 -144

121 Ibid, 145 -182

122 Ibid, 204 -234

123 Ibid, 235—260

124 Ibid, 261 -286

125 Ibid, 287-308

126 Charles Colson, 10

127 William Demas, *The Political Economy of the English-Speaking Caribbean: A Summary View,* CADEC, 1971.

128 Ibid

129 Carl F. Ellis, *Beyond Liberation : The Gospel of the Black American Experience,* InterVarsity Press, 1983

130 Francis Schaeffer, *True Spirituality,* Tyndale House Publishers, 1978, 63

131 Carl F. Ellis, 7

132 ibid, 7

133 Ibid, 23

[134]   Ibid, 27

[135]   Ibid, 43

[136]   Ibid, 44

[137]   Ibid, 44

[138]   Elwyn McQuilkin, *The Best of Wizard*, 2008

[139]   Angela Williams, *Harvest Praise 11*, Covenant People, 1988

[140]   Bob Marley, *Legend*, 1984, Island Records Ltd.

[141]   M. Scott Peck, *The Different Drum: Community—making and Peace,* Simon & Schuster, 1987, 17

[142]   Peter Block, *Stewardship: Choosing Service over Self-Interest,* Berrett-Koehler Publishers Inc., 1993, 228

[143]   M. Scott Peck, *The Different Drum,* 1987, 60

[144]   Ibid, 61-63

[145]   Ibid, 86

[146]   Ibid, 86-90

[147]   Ibid, 90-94

[148]   Ibid, 94-103

[149]   Ibid, 103-106

[150]   Joan Purcell, *Memoirs of a Woman in Politics: Spiritual Struggle,* Authorhouse, 2009, 309

[151] M. Scott Peck, *The Different Drum,* 1987, 317

[152] Ibid, 318

[153] Ibid, 104

[154] Ibid, 104

[155] Garnett Roper, "Caribbean Reading of Mark 5", Presentation CONECAR, Jamaica, 2009, 1

[156] H. P. Spees, "Evangelizing Young People in Different Cultures", Article prepared for Youth For Christ International, USA, 1993

[157] M. Scott Peck, *The Different Drum,* 1987, 324

[158] Francis A.Schaeffer & Udo W. Middelmann, *Pollution and the Death of Man: The Christian View of Ecology,* Good News Publications, 1992, 45/46

[159] Darrow L. Miller, Darrow L., *Discipling Nations: The Power of Truth to Transform Culture,* YWAM Publishing, 2001, 221

[160] Ibid, 225

[161] Ibid, 232

[162] Ibid, 229

[163] Ibid, 229

[164] Peter Block, 1993, 3

[165] Ibid, 5

[166] Ibid, 3

[167] Ibid, xxii

[168] Ibid, 49

[169] Jeremy Rifkin, *Entropy: A New World View,* Viking Press, 1980, *233/234*

[170] Ibid, 235

[171] Donald Dorr, *Spirituality and Justice,* 1984, 139.

[172] M. Scott Peck, *The Different Drum,* 1987, 17/74

[173] Darrow L. Miller, *Discipling Nations: The Power of Truth to Transform,* 2001, 200

[174] Ibid, 199

[175] Ibid 200

[176] Ibid 201

[177] Ibid, 201

[178] Ibid, 201 - 205

[179] Stephen Mansfield, *The Faith of Barack Obama,* Thomas Nelson, 2008

[180] Ibid, xv

[181] Tillich, Paul, *Dynamics of Faith,* Harper & Row, 1957

[182] James W. Fowler, *Becoming Adult, Becoming Christian: Adult Development and Christian Faith,* Harper & Row Publishers, 1984, 51

[183] Ibid, 1984, 50

[184] M. Scott Peck, *Further Along the Road Less Travelled: The Unending Journey toward Spiritual Growth,* Simon & Schuster, 1993

185 Ibid, 238

186 Ibid, 238

187 Ibid, 238

188 Ibid, 238

189 Francis Schaeffer, *Escape from Reason,* InterVarsity Press, 1968

190 Charles Colson, *Kingdoms in Conflict,* Hodder & Stoughton, 1989, 70

191 Charles C. Kao, *Search for Maturity,* The Westminister Pres, 1975, 50/51

192 W.J. Bouwsma, "Christian Adulthood" in Erikson, E.H. (Ed.) *Adulthood,* W.W. Norton & Co., 1978, 90

193 Fowler, 1984, 62

194 Ibid, 62

195 Ibid, 64

196 Ibid, 65

197 Mansfield, 2008, xvi

198 Ibid, 26/27

199 Clarke E. Moustakas, *Personal Growth: The Struggle for Identity* and Human Values, Doyle Publishing Co. 1969, ix

200 Keith Miller, *The Becomers,* Word Book Publishers, 1977

201 Joan Purcell, "Naked and Unashamed: A Journey into Faith & Maturity", 1986, 17/18

[202]   Fowler. 1984, 88

[203]   Mansfield, 2008, 121

[204]   Charles Colson, *Against the Night: Living in the New Dark Ages,* Servant
        Publications, 1989, 120

[205]   Charles Colson, *Kingdoms in Conflict,* Hodder & Stoughton, 1987 49

[206]   Ibid, 118

[207]   Ibid, 102

[208]   http://www.brainyquote.com/quotes/quotes/a/abrahamlin100844.html,
        08.11.10

[209]   http://www.brainyquote.com/quotes/quotes/a/abrahamlin100844.html,
        08.11.10

[210]   www.brainyquotes.com/quotes/quotes.abrahamkuy.190290.html, 08.11.10

[211]   Mansfield, 2001, 85

[212]   www.quotedb.com/quotes/66, 08.11.10

[213]   Curtiss Paul DeYoung, *Living Faith: How Faith inspires Social Justice,* Fortress
        Press, 2007, 121

[214]   Colson, *Kingdoms in Conflict,* 1987, 322/323

[215]   Nelson Mandela, *Long Walk to Freedom: The Autobiography of Nelson Mandela,*
        Little, Brown & Company, 1994, 495

[216]   Ibid, 544

[217]   Ibid, 544

[218] DeYoung, 2007, 103

[219] Robert C. Tucker, *Politics as Leadership,* University of Missouri Press, 1995, 2

[220] Ibid, 2

[221] Ibid, 9

[222] Ibid, 27

[223] Ibid, 31

[224] Ibid, 31

[225] M. Scott Peck, *A World Waiting to be Born: Civility Rediscovered,* Bantam Books, 1993, 61

[226] Ibid, 61

[227] Ibid, 5

[228] Ibid, 5

[229] Ibid, 53

[230] Ibid, 53

[231] Leonard Hulley, Louise & Pato Kretzchmar, Lungile Luke (EDS.), *Archbishop Tutu: Prophetic Witness in South Africa,* Human & Rousseau Ltd, 1996, 53

[232] Doug Bandow, Beyond Good Intentions: A Biblical View of Politics, Crossway Books, 1988, 15

[233] Kevin Rudd, "Faith in Politics", Online Monthly, 7/29/2008, 1

234   Ibid, 2

235   Ibid, 3

236   Ibid, 3

237   Ibid, 5

238   Ibid, 7

239   Bandow, 1988, 33

240   Jim Wallis, *The Soul of Politics,* 1995, xiii

241   Ibid, xiii

242   Ibid, xvi

243   Ibid, xvi

244   Garnett Roper, 2009, 3

245   Wallis, 1995, 46/47

246   In conversation with regional colleague May 2010

247   Robert C. Tucker, 11

248   Peter Block, *Stewardship,* 1993, 6

249   Blaine Lee, *The Power Principle: Influence with Honor,* Simon & Schuster, 1997, 274

250   Stephen Covey, *Principle-Centered Leadership,* Summit Books, 1990.

251   Blaine Lee, *The Power Principle: Influence with Honor,* 1997

252 M. Scott Peck, *A World Waiting to be Born: Civility Rediscovered, 1993*

253 Robert K. Greenleaf, *Servant Leadership: A Journey into the Nature of Legitimate Power and Greatness,* Paulist Press, 2002

254 M. Scott Peck, *A World waiting to be Born,* 5

255 Ibid, 53

256 Barack Obama in CNN telecast, Debates on Health Bill 2009

257 Charles F. Pfeiffer, Harrison, Everett F., (ED), *The Wycliffe Bible Commentary,* Moody Press, 1979, 968

258 Myles Munroe, *Becoming A Leader,* Pheuma Life Publishers, 1993, 10

259 Dan B. Allender, *Leading with a Limp: Turning Your Struggles into Strengths,* Waterbrook Press, 2006, 3

260 Ibid, 77

261 Ibid, 71—77

262 Ibid, 56

263 Ibid, 173

264 Ron Boehme, *Leadership for the 21st Century: Changing Nations through the Power of Serving,* YWAM Publishing, 1989

265 Robert K. Greenleaf, 2002, 24

266 Ibid, 27

267 Tom Marshall, *Understanding Leadership,* Sovereign World Ltd., 1991

[268] Gene C. Wilkes, *On Jesus Leadership,* Tyndale House Publishers, 1998, 217

[269] Ibid, 217

[270] M. Scott Peck, *The Different Drum,* 103

[271] Blaine Lee, 1997, 2

[272] Ibid, 292

[273] Stephen R. Covey, *Principle-Centered Leadership,* Summit Books, 1990, 284

[274] Ibid, 285

[275] Ibid, 287

[276] Blaine Lee, 1997, 294/5

[277] Ibid, 295

[278] Nelson Mandela, 1994, 574

[279] Wendy Grenade, 2009, 6

[280] Ibid, 6

[281] Ron Boehme, 1989, 15

[282] Ibid, 16

[283] Ibid, 14

[284] Ibid, 15

285   Darrow L. Miller, "Culture: Where the Physical & Spiritual Converge", 2009 Personal Prayer Diary Daily Planner, YWAM 2009, 20

286   Ibid 21

287   James R. Lucas, *Balance of Power*, AMACOM, 1998, 18 & 80

288   Ibid, 62

289   Ibid, 63

290   David Hinds, "Beyond Formal Democracy: The Discourse on Democracy and Governance in the Anglophone Caribbean", 2008, in *Commonwealth & Comparative Politics,* Volume 46, Issue 3, July 2008, 308-406.

291   Ibid, 314

292   DeYoung, 2007, 1 -10

293   Ibid, 7

294   Ibid, 8

295   Ibid, 8 &23

296   Ibid, 149

Bibliography

The King James Version (KJV)
The New King James Version (NKJV)
The New International Version (NIV)
The Amplified Version (AMP)
The Message (MSG)

Allender, Dan B. *Leading with a Limp: Turning Your Struggles into Strengths,* Waterbrook Press, 2006

Antrobus, Peggy, "The Empowerment of Women", Women and Development Unit, Barbados, 1989

Antrobus, Peggy, *The Global Women's Movement: Issues and Strategies for the New Century,* Zed Books, 2005.

Baker, Christopher, Resurrection Sunday Sermon,, April 20, 2010

Bandow, Doug, *Beyond Good Intentions: A Biblical View of Politics,* Crossway Books, 1988

Beckford, G. & Witter, M., *Small Garden, Bitter Weeds: Struggle and Change in Jamaica,* Zed Publishers, 1982

Bernard, A.R., Sunday Sermon, May 03, 2009, Christian Cultural Centre, Brooklyn, NY.

Block, Peter, *Stewardship: Choosing Service over Self-Interest,* Berrett-Koehler Publishers Inc., 1993

Boehme, Ron, *Leadership for the 21st Century: Changing Nations through the Power of Serving,* YWAM Publishing, 1989

Bouwsma, W.J., "Christian Adulthood" in Erikson, E.H. (Ed.) *Adulthood,* W.W. Norton & Co., 1978

Colson, Charles, *Against the Night: Living in the New Dark Ages,* Servant Publications, 1989

Colson, Charles, *Kingdoms in Conflict,* Hodder & Stoughton, 1987

Commissioner of Police, Jamaica, Statement on BBC Caribbean Report 10.05.2010

Conn, Harvie, M. *Evangelism: Doing Justice and preaching Grace,* Zondervan Publishing House, 1962

Covey, Stephen R., *Principle-centered Leadership,* Summit Books, 1990

Covey, Stephen, *Seven Habits of Highly Effective People,* Simon & Schuster, 1990

Crabb, Lawrence, *Inside Out,* NaviPress Publications, 1989

CWAL 1V, 274

Dawkins, Richard, *The God Delusion,* Bantam Press, 2006

De Allie, Christopher, Paper on "Global Economic Crisis and its Consequences for the Region", 2009

Demas, William, *The Political Economy of the English-Speaking Caribbean: A Summary View,* CADEC, 1971.

DeYoung, Curtiss Paul, *Living Faith: How Faith inspires Social Justice,* Fortress Press, 2007

Dorr, Donald, *Spirituality & Justice,* Orbis Books, New York, 1984

Ellis, Carl F., *Beyond Liberation: The Gospel of the Black American Experience,*

Intervarsity Press, 1983

Ellis, Pat, Conversation on Poverty in the communities, 2009

Food & Agriculture Organization, Paper presented on the Global Food Crisis: Implication for the Developing World, Sept.2009

Foster, Richard, *Money, Sex and Power: The Challenge of the Disciplined Life,* Hodder & Stoughton, 1985.

Fowler, *Becoming Adult, Becoming Christian: Adult Development and Christian Faith,* Harper & Row Publishers, 1984

Galtung, Johan, "Towards a New Economics: on the theory and practice of self-reliance" in *The Living Economy, Edited by Paul Ekins,* Routledge and Kenan Paul, 1986

Goulet, Dennis, *Cruel Choice: A New Concept in the Theory of Development,* Atheneum Books, 1971

Greenleaf, Robert K., *Servant Leadership,* Paulist, 1977

Grenade, Wendy C., "Democracy, Governance and Citizenship: A Community-Based Approach", Discussion Paper 2010

Grenade, Wendy, Feature Address at 20th Biennual Conference of the Soroptimist International of the Caribbean Network, "Reclaiming Communities through Service", August 2009

Henry-Wilson, Maxine, Paper on "The Poor and the Powerless", 1992

Hinds, David, "Beyond Formal Democracy: The Discourse on Democracy and Governance in the Anglophone Caribbean", 2008, in *Commonwealth & Comparative Politics,* Volume 46, Issue 3, July 2008, 308-406.

http://www.un.org/esa/sustdev/sids/sidslist.htm, accessed June 3, 2010

http://www.brainyquote.com/quotes/quotes/a/abrahamlin100844.html, 08.11.10

http://www.brainyquote.com/quotes/quotes/a/abrahamlin100844.html, 08.11.10

Hulley Leonard, Kretzchmar, Louise & Pato, Luke Lungile (EDS.), *Archbishop Tutu: Prophetic Witness in South Africa,* Human & Rousseau Ltd, 1996

Johnson, Darrell, W., *Discipleship on the Edge,* Regent College Publishing, Vancouver, British Columbia, 2004

Jones, D. Adele & Jemmott, Ena Trotman, "Report on Perception of Child Sexual Abuse in the Eastern Caribbean, 2009.

Kao, Charles C. *Search for Maturity,* The Westminister Pres, 1975

Kuhn, Thomas, *The Structure of Scientific Revolutions,* University of Chicago Press, 1962

Lausanne Covenant 1974

Lee, Blaine, *The Power Principle: Influence with Honor,* Simon & Schuster, 1997

Liebman, Joshua, *Peace of Mind,* Simon & Schuster, 1946

Lucas, James R., *Balance of Power,* AMACOM. 1998

Mandela, Nelson, *Long Walk to Freedom: The Autobiography of Nelson Mandela,* Little, Brown & Company, 1994

Mansfield, Stephen, *The Faith of Barack Obama,* Thomas Nelson, 2008

Marley, Bob, *Legend,* 1984, Island Records Ltd.

Marshall, Tom, *Understanding Leadership,* Sovereign World Ltd., 1991

Max-Neef, Manfred, "Human-scale economics: the challenges ahead" in *The Living Economy,* edited by Paul Ekins, Routledge and Kenan Paul, 1986

McAfee, Kathy, *Storm Signals: Structural Adjustment and Development Alternatives in the Caribbean,* Zed Books Ltd., 1991

McQuilkin, Elwyn, *The Best of Wizard,* 2008

Miller, Darrow L., *Discipling Nations, The Power of Truth to Transform Cultures, YWAM Publishing, 2001*

Miller, Darrow L., "Culture: Where the Physical & Spiritual Converge", article from forthcoming book on Biblical Theology and Vocation by YWAM Publishing, in 2009 Personal Prayer Diary, YWAM 2009

Miller Errol, *Men at Risk,* Jamaica Publishing House Ltd., 1991

Miller, Keith, *The Becomers,* Word Book Publishers, 1977

Moustakas, Clarke E., *Personal Growth: The Struggle for Identity* and Human Values, Doyle Publishing Co. 1969

Munroe, Myles, *Becoming A Leader,* Pheuma Life Publishers, 1993

Munroe, Myles, *The Burden of Freedom,* Charisma House, 2000

Nettleford, Rex M. *Caribbean Cultural identity: The Case of Jamaica,* Institute of Jamaica, 1978

Ostergaard, Lisa (ED), *Gender and Development,* Commission of the European Communities, 1992

Peck, M. Scott, *A World Waiting to be Born: Civility, Rediscovered,* Bantam Books, 1993

Peck, M. Scott, *Further Along the Road Less Travelled: The Unending Journey toward Spiritual Growth,* Simon & Schuster, 1993

Peck, M. Scott, *The Different Drum: Community-making and Peace,* Simon & Shuster, NY, 1987

Pfeiffer, Charles F., Harrison, Everett F., (ED), *The Wycliffe Bible Commentary,* Moody Press, 1979

President of Guyana, TV Interview on Caribbean News Service, May 25, 2009

Purcell, Joan, *Memoirs of a Woman in Politics: Spiritual Struggle,* Authorhouse, 2009

Purcell, Joan, "Naked and Unashamed: A Journey into Faith & Maturity", 1986.

Rifkin, Jeremy, *Entrophy: A New World View,* Viking Press, 1980

Roche, Neville, "Book Review of Joan Purcell's Memoirs", 2009

Roper, Garnett, "Caribbean Reading of Mark 5", Presentation CONECAR, Jamaica, 2009

Rudd, Kevin, "Faith in Politics", Online Monthly, 7/29/2008

Schaeffer, Francis, *Escape from Reason,* InterVarsity Press, 1968

Schaeffer, Francis, *How Should we then live? The Rise and Decline of Western Thought and Culture,* Crossway Books, 1984

Schaeffer, Francis, *Pollution and the Death of Man: The Christian View of Ecology,* 1970

Schaeffer, Francis, *True Spirituality*, Tyndale House Publishers, 1978

Spees, H.P., "Evangelizing Young People in Different Cultures", Article prepared for Youth For Christ International, USA, 1993

Storkey, Elaine, *What's Right with Feminism,* Eerdmans Publishing Co., 1985

Stott, John, *Issues Facing Christians Today,* Marshall, Morgan & Scott, 1984

Tillich, Paul, *Dynamics of Faith,* Harper & Row, 1957

Tucker, Robert C., *Politics as Leadership,* University of Missouri Press, 1995, 2

UN Department of Social Affairs, Division of Sustainable Development, "What are the SIDS?"—Internet, 2007

UNICEF, "Situation Analysis of Women and Children in the Eastern Caribbean" 2007

Venner, Dwight, Feature Address at the Launch of a Public Consultation process on the Establishment of the OECS Economic Union, March 2009

Wallis, Jim, *The Soul of Politics; Beyond "Religious Right" and "Secular Left",* Harcourt, Brace & Company, 1995

Wilkes, Gene C., *On Jesus Leadership,* Tyndale House Publishers, 1998

Williams, Angela, *Harvest Praise 11*, Covenant People, 1988

Witter, Michael, *Social Change: Christian and Social Science Perspectives*, edited by Mark Figueroa and Judith Soares, Department of Economics, UWI, Jamaica, Monograph # 3

www.brainyquotes.com/quotes/quotes . . . abrahamkuy.190290.html, 08.11.10